D1586397

Welcome

THERE'S ONE FUNDAMENTAL CHANGE between Windows Vista and Windows XP that's passed almost everyone by. Microsoft, it seems, has become a people company.

It's paid lip service before. 'My Computer' sat proudly on the Desktop when you booted up your Windows XP PC, but that just left most people feeling vaguely patronised. Likewise, dogs wagging their tails as they searched for your files, a metaphor that should have been put to sleep. In Vista, all that's swept away. This is a far more sophisticated operating system, which, with a bit of tweaking, you can adjust to your way of working.

The big-ticket item, though, is security. After all the unwelcome headlines about security holes in Windows XP, Microsoft has made safety the foundation on which everything else is built. In practice, this means built-in phishing detection for Internet Explorer (so, if you're directed to a website that only *looks* like Barclays Bank, it should be stopped in its tracks), anti-spyware software as standard, a beefed-up firewall and some highly advanced parental controls.

But in many ways, the difference between Vista and XP is summed up by the screen that greets you on start-up (see our at-a-glance guide on p38). Rather than a Teletubbies landscape, you're presented with a stylish backdrop and an understated analogue clock. No more primary colours: now the tones are muted and attractive.

It turns out that Windows has grown up and, although we're still not 100% satisfied with this release, it's undoubtedly the finest operating system Microsoft has ever produced. On p8, you'll find eight instant reasons to upgrade. Keep on reading to discover our complete practical guide to how you can do it and why you should.

Tim Danton, Editor
editor@pcpro.co.uk

Lenovo recommends Windows Vista™ Business.

Windows Vista
Business

A LITTLE BIT BOARDROOM.
A LITTLE BIT BAD BOY.

It's a battle-tested business machine. It's a titanium-covered widescreen statement. It's pre-loaded with Windows Vista™.* It's a notebook for both sides of your brain. The Lenovo ThinkPad® notebook.
New World. New Thinking.™

lenovo

lenovo.com/microsoft/uk

CONTENTS

Lenovo recommends Windows Vista™ Business.

Designed for
Windows® XP

Windows Vista™
Capable

TURN HEADS.

Take notes. Get noticed.
The Lenovo ThinkPad X60 Tablet
PC, powered by Windows® XP
Tablet PC Edition and Windows
Vista™ Premium Ready. It's a
drawing pad. It's a note pad.
Best of all, it's a ThinkPad.
New World. New Thinking.™

lenovo.com/microsoft/uk

BBC - Comedy & Drama **7**
The best of BBC comedy, drama and books

Windows Meeting Space **10**

8

11

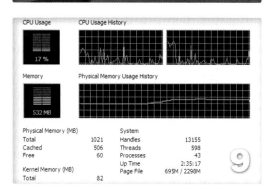

9

Working with files and folders

12

CONTENTS

CHAPTERS
7-12

88 CHAPTER 7
LEISURE & ENTERTAINMENT
Vista is the best operating system ever for digital entertainment. With the Windows Media Center built in, it's all you need for music, films and TV – and it's great for games, too. Here's how to make the most of it.

102 CHAPTER 8
STAYING SAFE IN VISTA
Hackers, viruses and spyware are a huge problem. Vista has tough new measures to deal with them, plus added protection with comprehensive parental controls.

118 CHAPTER 9
TUNING UP VISTA
By default, Vista sets itself up to be optimised for the average user. But who's average? See if you can benefit from some basic tweaks and enhancements.

128 CHAPTER 10
HOME NETWORKING
Bought a brand new PC with Vista pre-installed? Then you can set up a network to share files with your old Windows XP system in just a few minutes. Follow our step-by-step guides to learn how.

138 CHAPTER 11
ON THE MOVE
Laptop users will benefit most of all from Vista, with better power management, more reliable sleep modes and the all-new Mobility Center. Find out more here.

150 CHAPTER 12
WINDOWS HELP
When things go wrong (and, with computers, they will), there are excellent support tools in Vista. Here's our guide to getting quick and accurate answers...

Eight reasons to up

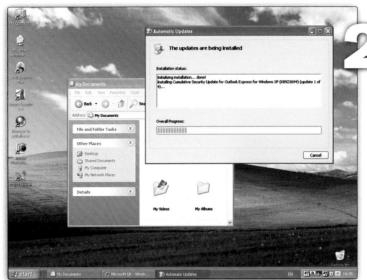

A GROWN-UP OS Remember this? Sorry, you're probably faced with it every day. Well, the Fisher-Price look derided by Apple and Linux fans is history. Gaudy colours are replaced with pastels, clunky corners have been rounded, and every surface and edge has a smooth look. But, even more important than the metaphorical fresh lick of paint, the operating system itself is now much easier to use. For instance, where we'd rarely have advised anyone to use the networking wizards in Windows XP, we'd advise everyone – except perhaps the odd wizened IT consultant – to use the setup assistants provided by Vista. We also appreciate the inclusion of a fully fledged backup program that's so easy to use, people actually will.

BEEFY SECURITY Microsoft is determined not to repeat XP's security shortcomings. Bill Gates says it's 'dramatically more secure than any other operating system released', and for once there's justification for the hype. If your PC is behind a router, which usually includes an effective hardware firewall, there's enough additional security built into Vista to avoid spending more money on an internet security suite. It isn't bullet-proof, though, so read Chapter 8, 'Staying safe in Vista' (see p102).

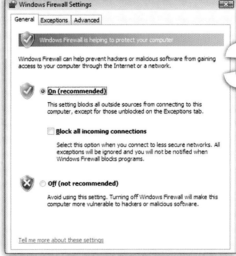

FIND FILES INSTANTLY Most computers contain thousands of files, arranged in a way that seemed terribly logical at the time – the computing equivalent of that 'safe place' you put something last week. Imagine a world where you just type a keyword or two and, within a second, a shortlist of relevant documents appears. That's just the beginning of Vista's abilities. If you master its advanced search capabilities, and especially if you start to add keyword tags to files like photos and videos, you'll soon be able to locate every single document you create within milliseconds rather than minutes.

FAQ

Q **So is there anything that Windows XP did better?**

A There are a few things you might miss from XP. Quite apart from familiarity – we've been using XP for five years, after all – the menu system was less fiddly. Vista does have a habit of adding drop-down menus in places where you don't really expect drop-down menus to be, often at the expense of good old-fashioned menu bars at the top.

QUICK LAUNCH Our favourite feature isn't the flash new interface, it isn't the improved security, it isn't the fact that most of the bundled programs are now actually very good. It's Vista's ability to launch programs with five (or fewer) keystrokes. Press the Windows key, type 'calc', and Calculator will instantly launch. If you use Microsoft Word, 'word' will open it. No hunting through menus, no need even to pick up the mouse. It may not sound revolutionary, but it makes for a much more enjoyable day-to-day experience.

grade to Vista today

5 **LITTLE THINGS** There are lots of tiny apps in Vista that make life a little bit more enjoyable. Things like a chess game that's actually quite good (see p100); a by-the-month calendar that springs into view when you click on the clock in the Taskbar (see p78); a photo gallery program that displays photos the way you always wanted them displayed, even though you never knew it (see p80). These mini-programs, which in some cases can claim to be fully fledged applications, are light years ahead of their equivalents in Windows XP. Although we'd never claim they're so brilliant you should upgrade instantly just for them, they're the sort of hidden extra that make you rather glad you did.

6 **BIG THINGS** You needn't look too far to find the big-ticket apps bundled with Vista, and the undisputed chief is Media Center. Although there was a version of Windows XP that included Media Center, it never hit the mainstream and never really deserved to: it was too clunky, and (until the very last version) too difficult to get working. The Media Center experience in Vista is miles better. Since Vista resumes from standby in just a couple of seconds, you can switch it on almost as quickly as you can a TV. It's now actually a pleasure to browse your music collection, as you simply sweep through all your album covers, and you can even record TV and then burn it to DVD – all from your sofa if you prefer.

7 **RUN WINDOWS YOUR WAY** This is the most customisable version of Windows ever. It's now quick and easy to set up different accounts for every member of the family and apply parental controls. It's equally simple to change your Desktop background, colour scheme and 'theme' (expect lots of downloadable themes to appear). Change the way folders display to suit the way you work. And you can go much further, thanks to the new Sidebar with your choice of Gadgets. Set one clock for New York and one for London; show the weather for where you live; use onscreen sticky notes – your choices are endless.

8 **SAVE MONEY** We've mentioned the reduced need for expensive security suites: adding virus protection is the only essential, and on p108 we explain how to do this for free. You may also be able to save money on electricity. Since XP's Standby mode was unreliable, many people kept their PCs running all day. Vista's renamed Sleep mode works extremely well, and leaps back into action a couple of seconds after you prod the mouse. By default, Vista goes into Sleep mode after an hour of being idle, but be a bit tougher with your power settings and you'll save even more.

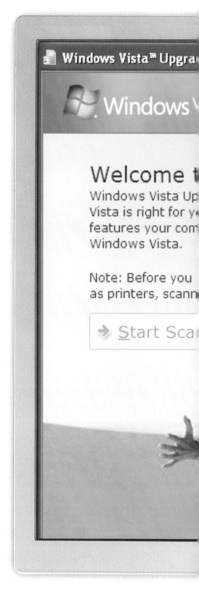

12 **How to... Use Vista Upgrade Advisor**
Microsoft provides a free utility to analyse your current PC and see if installing Vista will be successful.

16 **Upgrading a notebook for Vista**
Many notebooks will be able to run Vista quite capably, but there are a couple of upgrades you may need.

14 **Choosing the right Vista for you**
Windows Vista comes in different editions for home, business and power users. Which should you pick?

18 **Upgrading a desktop PC for Vista**
Your PC may be compatible with Vista, but a few extra tweaks could help you get the most out of it.

CHAPTER 1

GETTING READY

The good news: if your current computer can run Windows XP, it's very likely that it will also be able to run Windows Vista. The bad news: you might need to increase the amount of memory in your computer, while your current graphics card may not be able to take advantage of all the fancy new visual effects. But never fear. In this chapter, we provide a detailed

Advisor 1.0

Upgrade Advisor

Windows Vista Upgrade Advisor

ade Advisor will scan your computer to help you choose which edition of Windows
. It will also provide guidance about many of the advanced Windows Vista
ter supports and compatibility of your existing software and devices with

art the scan, plug in any devices that you regularly use with your computer, such
s, or external hard drives.

FOR VISTA

breakdown of how to determine exactly how Vista-
ready your system really is, and we reveal how to
carry out all of the vital upgrades you're most likely
to need, whether it's your notebook's memory or your
PC's graphics card. By the end, you should know
exactly what steps you need to take to get your current
computer prepared to run Vista.

HOW LONG?
Ten minutes, once
you've downloaded
the software.

HOW HARD?
Easy – the only
difficulty may be in
finding updates.

HOW TO...
USE VISTA UPGRADE ADVISOR

To make it as simple as possible to upgrade to Windows Vista, Microsoft has provided a free tool called the Vista Upgrade Advisor. This analyses your current PC and reveals any potential problems you might encounter during installation.

1 **DOWNLOAD THE ADVISOR** First, you need to download the Windows Vista Upgrade Advisor software. Either go to www.microsoft.com and enter the term 'upgrade advisor' into the search box at the top right of the home page, or enter this full address to go directly to the Upgrade Advisor download page: www.microsoft.com/windowsvista/getready/upgradeadvisor/default.mspx. Note that the Advisor only works with Windows XP (the 32-bit edition, not the 64-bit edition) and it's a 6.6MB download. Click on the download link, then select Run.

2 **RUN THE APPLICATION** Once the Advisor is downloaded, it should run automatically. If you see a Security Warning pop up, however, click Run. Once it's installed, you should see an icon on your Desktop. You'll then be greeted with the Welcome screen, and you can click Start Scan. It's important to ensure that any devices you depend upon (in particular, external drives, memory sticks, printers or scanners) are plugged in at this point, as the Advisor will then be able to check for the drivers they'll require. We also recommend that your computer is connected to the internet during the whole process.

3 **THE SCANNING PROCESS** It'll take a minute or two for the Vista Upgrade Advisor to scan your computer, and you can browse some basic information about the different versions of Windows Vista while you wait. Behind the scenes, the Upgrade Advisor is determining the exact hardware and software configuration of your computer, and then comparing it to an online database that contains information on all the available Vista drivers.

4 **VIEW THE RESULTS** When the scan has finished, follow the prompts and you'll be shown a summary of the results – hopefully saying you can run Vista. The Advisor will also recommend a Vista version suitable for your PC, with links that detail the different features the recommended version will support. If you're interested in a particular feature (for example, Windows Aero with Flip 3D), click on the link and you'll be taken to the relevant website.

5 **CHECK THE DETAILS** If you scroll down the page, however, you're likely to be greeted with a yellow triangle warning you of possible issues. Stay calm! This doesn't mean you won't be

able to run Vista on your computer, it merely highlights the possibility that certain components of your system would benefit from upgrades or new drivers. The Advisor breaks down these results into three key areas: System Requirements, which covers the most significant components, such as your PC's processor; Devices, such as the sound card; and Programs, such as Windows Messenger. You can click on See Details to get further information on each area.

6 SYSTEM DETAILS Here we've clicked the See Details button for System Requirements. In the case of our computer – an IBM ThinkPad laptop – Vista Advisor is recommending that we upgrade to a DVD drive. This is simply because Windows Vista is supplied on a DVD rather than CDs (although CDs are available on request). You may also be advised that you need to upgrade your 'video card', more commonly known as a graphics card in the UK, to take advantage of the all-new Windows Aero experience (see p46). There's also a link to a list of video cards that support Aero to help you decide what you might upgrade to.

In our example, we're also recommended to upgrade our memory. If you have anything less than 1GB of RAM currently installed, the Upgrade Advisor will give you this message too. Although you can get away with 512MB of memory, you may find that Vista doesn't run as quickly as you'd like. Vista is far more forgiving when it comes to processor speed. Provided that your CPU (your computer's main processor) runs at a modest 800MHz or faster, you'll be advised that 'No action' is required – in other words, you don't need to upgrade your processor.

7 DEVICES AND PROGRAMS We're told that our ThinkPad's TrackPoint mouse substitute and the wireless networking card we've installed won't work under Vista with their current drivers. It's likely you'll be faced with some similar messages for your system. At this point, you should head to the support section of the manufacturer's website for your computer, or for the individual component, and try a search using suitable keywords. In our case, 'vista wireless 2100 3b' returned the correct driver for the wireless card at www.intel.com. You may also discover that your manufacturer has set up a specific website for Vista queries, complete with a list of available downloads. Finally, take careful note of any programs the Upgrade Advisor declares incompatible with Windows Vista. Many will just require an update, but some may never be compatible; you'll either have to buy a new version, or decide whether or not you can live without that program. For example, Nero 6 has a serious conflict with Vista, and lots of security software will generate similar warnings. It could well be, however, that the built-in DVD-burning and security software provided by Vista itself (see p84 and p102 respectively) are perfectly suitable for your needs.

8 CHECK THE TASK LIST Click on Task List and you'll be presented with a full guide to what you need to do before and after you install Windows Vista. This is an aggregation of the other three pages (System, Devices and Programs) into one handy page, complete with a summary of your system. It's well worth printing this out (simply click the Print task list button, at the top right of the page) or saving the report (again, click the button or link) as a web page.

TIP

▶ Once you've determined what drivers or software updates need to be applied after you've installed Vista, we recommend you download and save the drivers to a USB memory stick or external hard disk – making sure that they're Vista-compatible according to the Advisor – so they're ready straight away. Alternatively, keep a network cable to hand for after the installation so that you can connect to the internet and get the downloads even if, for example, wireless drivers are required.

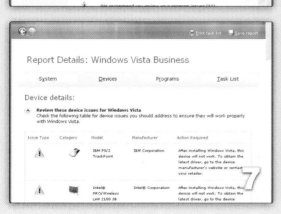

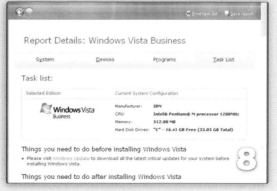

WINDOWS VISTA IS AVAILABLE IN A CONFUSING RANGE OF VERSIONS, BUT
A LITTLE INVESTIGATION WILL REVEAL WHICH ONE YOU SHOULD PICK.

Choosing the right Vista for you

For the home user, there were only two versions of Windows XP to consider: Home and Professional. The lines between them were pretty clearly drawn, with XP Home suitable for 90% of home users, while XP Professional catered for the 10% of enthusiasts who wanted more advanced features such as better networking tools.

Vista makes things a little more complicated: there are eight different versions in all. Of these, however, two editions won't be available to buy off the shelf in the UK: Vista Starter will be confined to markets in developing countries, and Vista Enterprise to large businesses. Vista Business is aimed at the small to medium business, so this leaves the home user with a choice of three editions: Home Basic, Home Premium and Ultimate.

The sharp-witted will have noticed that's a total of six rather than eight. The missing two are Home Basic N and Business N, which don't include Windows Media Player. They only exist to appease the European Union, which was concerned that Microsoft had an unfair advantage over other creators of music players, such as RealPlayer. They're very unlikely ever to be offered for sale, so you can safely ignore them.

Windows Vista Home Basic edition doesn't include Media Center (above) or advanced graphics effects such as live previews, but is still a suitable choice for many home users.

Home Basic also incorporates the very comprehensive Parental Control features (see p110), making it a sensible choice for kids with their own PC in the bedroom to handle basic homework, internet research and email.

But Home Basic doesn't give you the pretty full Aero interface with its translucent Aero Glass windows, the Flip 3D task switcher, or the very useful thumbnail previews when you hover over an icon in the taskbar. It also lacks most of the entertainment features of the more expensive editions, most notably Windows Media Center. The final omission of note is that the Backup utility doesn't offer scheduling or backup to a network.

VISTA HOME BASIC

The cheapest of the editions commercially available in this country, Home Basic offers the revamped innards of Windows Vista but less of the glossy outside frippery. Its main benefits over Windows XP are the two mainstays of Vista: its enhanced security and the new focus on finding what you're looking for with fast, powerful search capabilities.

The idea is that Home Basic is a cheap edition of Vista for those staples of modern home computing, email and the internet. It includes Internet Explorer 7, of course, and integrated applications including the very capable Windows Mail (see p76) and Windows Calendar (see p78). You also get some extras in the form of the Windows Sidebar and its associated Gadgets (see p50).

On the security side of things, Home Basic gives you just as much protection as the other versions. It has the new UAC (user account control, see p42), making it harder for unauthorised programs to run without your consent; the new two-way Windows Firewall, which blocks both nasties trying to get in and nasties trying to get out; the revamped Windows Defender, to catch spyware and adware in your browser; and the malicious-software removal tool, which acts as a basic virus scanner.

VISTA HOME PREMIUM

Home Premium is the edition that most home users will end up buying, and the one most likely to be included if you buy a new Vista PC. It's roughly the equivalent of the old Windows XP Home Edition, but includes more extras.

The most immediately noticeable feature that Home Premium gives you over Home Basic is the full Aero interface, which takes advantage of modern graphics cards to allow the very sexy-looking new translucent windows. This assumes your PC has a graphics card or integrated graphics adaptor powerful enough, of course, but the good news is that most graphics cards made in the last couple of years will be able to cope pretty easily (see p18 and p23 for more on this). And in addition most laptops now have powerful enough integrated hardware to cope.

Other Aero enhancements include the Flip 3D task switcher and live thumbnail previews, which give you an idea of the contents of minimised windows when you hover your mouse over them in the Taskbar.

There's a lot more to Home Premium than that, though. First off, it comes with the full Windows Media Center application, which, unlike Windows Media Player (included with Home Basic), is a complete home entertainment 'front end' that takes over the screen display with its own set-top-box-style user interface. With Media Center installed, you can watch and record live TV (provided your PC has the necessary tuner hardware), play movies and view photos from the comfort of your armchair using a Media Center remote control.

Several of the applications included in Home Basic have extended features under Premium. Windows Photo Gallery, for instance, gains the ability to produce slide shows set to music. Perhaps more interesting are the extended capabilities of the built-in Backup application: with Home Premium you can schedule backups to run at regular times, and also back up to a network location, such as another PC on your home network.

For laptop users, Home Premium is the sensible choice because it features the Mobility Center, making portable-specific features easy to get to (see p140). You can also organise meetings using Windows Meeting Space (see p132), whereas Home Basic only allows you to join existing meetings.

VISTA ULTIMATE At the top of the tree – whether you're a home user, a professional user or even a large business – is Windows Vista Ultimate edition. Ultimate includes all the features from every other edition of Vista, including the Business and Enterprise editions, and adds a few more exclusive ones of its own. Perhaps the most tantalising of these is the Windows Ultimate Extras feature. This will allow you to download and access special extra applications and features as and when they're released by Microsoft, which won't be available to users of other editions. Initially the Ultimate Extras include the swish Dream Scene add-on to animate your desktop wallpaper; an extra game in the form of Texas Hold Em Poker; an extra tool to streamline preparing your hard disk for BitLocker drive encryption (see below); and the fascinating Group Shot application to allow you to stitch together the best parts of several photos to produce the perfect picture from your party snaps..

For more security-conscious users, and particularly those with lots of sensitive data on their laptops, one of the most attractive features of Vista Ultimate edition will be the BitLocker drive encryption system. Unlike standard folder encryption (available in Vista Business edition), BitLocker encrypts the entire contents of your hard disk, scrambling the data and rendering it completely inaccessible to anyone who steals your laptop or, potentially, the PC from your office or home.

BitLocker also has the option to use a standard USB flash drive as a physical hardware key. If the correct key isn't inserted in the PC, the machine is completely locked out.

WHAT'S IN EACH EDITION

	Home Basic	Home Premium	Ultimate edition
Price	£180	£220	£370
Upgrade price	£100	£150	£250

USER INTERFACE

	Home Basic	Home Premium	Ultimate edition
Aero experience	●	○	○
Instant Search	○	○	○
Live Preview	●	○	○
Windows Flip	○	○	○
Windows Flip 3D	●	○	○

BUNDLED APPS & GAMES

	Home Basic	Home Premium	Ultimate edition
Windows Calendar	○	○	○
Windows Contacts	○	○	○
Windows DVD Maker	●	○	○
Windows Fax and Scan	●	●	○
Windows Mail	○	○	○
Windows Movie Maker	○	○	○
Windows Movie Maker with HD support	●	○	○
Windows Photo Gallery	●	○	○
Windows Media Player	○	○	○

ENTERTAINMENT

	Home Basic	Home Premium	Ultimate edition
Chess Titans	●	○	○
FreeCell, Minesweeper, Solitaire	○	○	○
Inkball (Tablet PC game)	●	○	○
Mahjong Titans	●	○	○
Media Center Extender support	●	○	○
Windows Media Center	●	○	○

SECURITY & BACKUP

	Home Basic	Home Premium	Ultimate edition
BitLocker	●	●	○
Backup scheduling	●	○	○
Backup to network	●	○	○
Encrypting File System	●	●	○
Restore lost/edited files with Shadow Copy	●	●	○
Windows Complete PC Backup & Restore	●	●	○
Windows Defender	○	○	○
Windows Firewall	○	○	○

PERFORMANCE

	Home Basic	Home Premium	Ultimate edition
64-bit processor support	○	○	○
Maximum RAM (32-bit edition)	4GB	4GB	4GB
Maximum RAM (64-bit edition)	8GB	16GB	128GB
SMP support	●	○	○
Windows ReadyBoost	○	○	○

NOTEBOOK & TABLET PC

	Home Basic	Home Premium	Ultimate edition
Presentation mode (Mobility Center)	●	○	○
Tablet PC support	●	○	○
Windows Touch Technology	●	○	○

NETWORKING

	Home Basic	Home Premium	Ultimate edition
Meeting Space (ability to join)	○	○	○
Meeting Space (ability to organise)	●	○	○
Offline files and folders	●	●	○
Remote Desktop (ability to join)	○	○	○
Remote Desktop (ability to organise)	●	●	○

All prices from www.amazon.co.uk and correct at time of going to press, including VAT.

THERE'S EVERY CHANCE YOUR NOTEBOOK IS CAPABLE OF RUNNING VISTA.
HERE'S WHAT YOU NEED TO CHECK AND HOW TO UPGRADE.

Upgrading a notebook for Vista

Notebooks bring a number of unique challenges when it comes to upgrading to Windows Vista. The most obvious hurdle is processor speed: with Vista demanding a minimum 800MHz processor, almost every notebook that's more than four years old will struggle to cope with the new OS. You may also find that your hard disk falls short of Microsoft's 20GB recommendation. However, it is just possible to squeeze Vista onto a 10GB hard disk.

Yet another hurdle comes in the form of the optical drive. If your notebook only came with a CD drive, you'll need to buy a DVD drive simply to be able to read the DVD installation disc, unless you can ask Microsoft to send you a set of CDs (good luck). You can upgrade an optical drive, but it's a fiddly process and you should first check that it's possible to remove the existing drive. If it is, head over to a price comparison site such as www.froogle.co.uk and enter 'DVD drive notebook OEM' (without quote marks) to find a selection of DVD drives.

It's almost certain that you won't be able to upgrade your notebook's graphics card, which could mean that you won't be able to get the full Aero experience (see p46). This isn't a disaster, as Vista looks a huge amount better than Windows XP even without Aero – but if you do want features such as live preview, your best option is to offload your current notebook.

ADDING MEMORY Fortunately, the most obvious upgrade – memory – is relatively simple. Almost every notebook has an easily accessible memory socket, normally on the underside of the chassis. You may need to dispose of the memory that's already there in order to free the slot for a new, higher-capacity module, but at current prices of around £40 for 512MB SODIMMs (notebook memory modules, as opposed to DIMMs for desktop PC memory), that's not a great loss.

Make sure you're buying the right type of memory for your notebook. The simplest way to ensure this is to visit a supplier's site (try www.crucial.com/uk, www.kingston.com or www.corsairmemory.com) and select your exact model of notebook. As with desktop PCs, you should make sure no electricity is being fed to the memory socket when you upgrade. Remove the power supply and battery before you do anything else.

HOTKEY SUPPORT One final consideration is that you may lose some of the functions offered by the hotkeys built into your notebook's keyboard – for example, to control sound volume. There's little incentive for smaller notebook manufacturers to upgrade the software that makes these keys work. Before you install Vista, check the maker's support website for any such updates.

 TIP

▶ If you decide to upgrade your hard disk, you'll suddenly have a perfectly good 'old' hard disk on your hands. So why not put it to use? Buy a 2.5in hard disk enclosure (sometimes called a caddy) and you'll be able to use it as an external USB hard disk. PC Pro recently put four to the test (www.pcpro.co.uk/reviews/92157), and a Dynamode caddy costing less than £10 won a Recommended award.

Adding memory to a notebook is usually a straightforward process, but make sure you buy the right type of module for your model – and that you remove the battery before you add it.

HOW TO...
UPGRADE YOUR NOTEBOOK'S HD

It's true that upgrading a notebook's hard disk is a more complex task than it would be with a desktop PC, but it's by no means beyond the scope of most computer users. Here's how to get it right in four steps.

1 **REMOVE THE OLD DRIVE** Before you start, make a backup (see p26), as one misplaced screwdriver could lose all your data. Next, ensuring that the battery is removed and the power supply disconnected, remove your notebook hard disk. There may be a screw or two holding it in place. Some older notebooks don't allow you to remove the hard disk at all, as you may discover at this point. Assuming that it's possible, you'll soon have a combination of drive caddy and hard disk in your hands. Undo all the relevant screws and prise the hard disk gently from the caddy, using a flat-edged screwdriver if necessary.

2 **IDENTIFY THE INTERFACE** Unless you bought your notebook in the last year, it will almost certainly use a Parallel ATA hard disk. This refers to the type of connector, with two sets of gold-coloured pins being used to transfer data and power. New notebooks use SATA connectors as shown here, which are less fragile and generally offer faster transfer rates. Unless you know your notebook uses a SATA disk, buy a Parallel ATA disk. The PC Pro Recommended notebook hard disk is currently the 160GB Western Digital Scorpio, which costs around £60. See www.pcpro.co.uk/reviews/90549 for the review.

3 **INSERT THE NEW DRIVE** Now you need to insert your new disk into the notebook's hard disk caddy. We've pictured the IDE connector here as well, but this may be fixed in position within the notebook itself, so don't worry if you didn't remove it in Step 1. However, do make sure that the pins on the hard disk will be sliding into the correct connectors when you attempt to connect the new hard disk.

4 **INSTALL VISTA** Reconnect the battery and power supply, and start the Windows installation process as normal (see p28). Once this has completed, open Computer and check the size of the C: drive – this should correspond to the formatted capacity of the drive you installed. This is normally around 90% to 95% of the disk's nominal capacity, so for example a '160GB' drive will typically appear as a 150GB drive in Windows. If you can't access the whole of the disk, your notebook's BIOS may not support the full capacity. Check the notebook manufacturer's website for a BIOS update. If your notebook won't recognise your new hard disk at all, you may need to follow the notebook manufacturer's instructions to enter its BIOS and change the hard disk settings. You'll almost certainly get the best results by using the Auto option.

HOW LONG?
A couple of hours, including the time to back up your data.

HOW HARD?
It's not a difficult upgrade, but take care with the connectors.

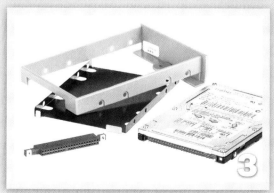

HERE'S HOW TO CHECK IF YOUR DESKTOP PC IS READY FOR VISTA, AND TACKLE
THE UPGRADES THAT MAY BE NECESSARY OR MERELY DESIRABLE TO RUN IT.

Upgrading a PC for Vista

Once you've run the Vista Upgrade Advisor (see p12), you should have a list of potential problems and a rough guide to solving them. Unlike a notebook, your PC should be upgradable in almost every aspect and, with a little knowledge and confidence, the upgrades are fairly easy.

It's unlikely that the processor will prove a problem: all that Vista requires is an 800MHz CPU, and even PCs dating from 2000 usually meet that specification. If your processor is slower than 800MHz, you should really buy a new computer rather than trying to upgrade.

Two core components that may well benefit from an upgrade are your hard disk and your memory, and we provide a step-by-step guide to those jobs over the next three pages. The graphics card is a more complex question.

UPGRADING GRAPHICS The most significant graphical difference between Windows XP and Vista is the Aero experience (see p46), which requires a decent level of 3D power from the graphics card. As long as your PC's card supports DirectX 9, you should have no problems running Aero, even at high resolutions. But the amount of memory your graphics card has dedicated to it also plays a part; we'd recommend at least 128MB. You may be able to get away with 64MB, but only if your CPU is significantly faster than the minimum requirement.

Bear in mind that a considerable number of graphics cards – especially entry-level models which use HyperMemory (on ATi cards) or TurboCache (on Nvidia cards) – have little memory of their own, instead borrowing a chunk of main memory (RAM). This is fine, as long as enough system RAM is being allocated for use by the graphics card; this is usually configurable in the BIOS.

We tried a variety of cards with 128MB of RAM, including an integrated Intel GMA 950 graphics chip and an Nvidia GeForce 6600 GT. All ran Vista's Aero, Flip 3D and Live Preview (where an application's thumbnail shows live video or animation). But, while the effects worked, not all were super-smooth. For example, with integrated graphics we could select the Aero theme, but Flip 3D was jerky and any videos playing in the live preview stuttered.

If your card is borderline, your best bet could be to stick with it for now, and upgrade later if Vista struggles.

OTHER UPGRADES Vista Home Premium includes Media Center (see p90), so if you have access to a TV aerial connection there's a strong argument for adding a TV tuner to your PC. Digital tuners, which let you watch Freeview channels such as BBC Four, cost around £55. If you have only basic budget speakers, as little as £30 will buy a much better set such as Logitech's X-230.

TIP

▶ Before you perform any upgrades on your PC, disconnect the power lead, then press the PC's power button to discharge any remaining electricity. Before touching any component, discharge any static energy from your body. You can do this by touching a central heating radiator or cold water tap, or buy an anti-static wristband.

TIP

▶ Never use excessive force when fitting RAM – you could break a memory module or, even worse, your motherboard. Firm pressure may be needed, but not brute force.

Take advantage of Vista's Media Center features by installing a digital TV tuner card, allowing you to watch Freeview channels via an aerial.

HOW TO...
UPGRADE YOUR PC'S MEMORY

Microsoft recommends 1GB of RAM to ensure Vista runs smoothly, and our experience confirms this. Fitting extra memory isn't difficult in itself, but choosing the right chips can be tricky. Here's our guide to avoiding the pitfalls.

1 **FIND THE RIGHT MEMORY** Crucial (www.crucial.com/uk) has built a nifty System Scanner just for people considering an upgrade to Vista. Click on the green Am I Vista Ready? button on the home page, then Scan My System. Once the scan is finished, click the yellow Get Help Upgrading button and you'll be taken to a page that shows your system specification – and even reveals whether you have any spare memory sockets. Follow the on-screen instructions to discover and order the right memory for your system.

2 **CHECK FOR DUAL-CHANNEL SUPPORT** Check in your motherboard's manual to see if it supports a dual-channel mode. Such boards typically have memory slots arranged in coloured pairs, as seen here, and will run faster if each pair of slots contains identical sticks of memory. DDR and DDR2 memory (see Glossary) is often sold in matched pairs for this reason.

3 **INSTALL YOUR NEW RAM** Memory is easy to install, but must be handled with care. Before you start, discharge any static electricity (see Tip, opposite page) and disconnect your PC's power and peripherals. Handle memory sticks by the edges of their circuit boards to avoid damage. If you're replacing existing memory, remove it by pressing down on the plastic retaining catches at each end of the slot. It's best to release both at once. Each slot will have one or two plastic ridges along its length, which stop you inserting the wrong kind of memory. If your motherboard isn't dual-channel (see Step 2), it may have two, three or four slots. You should usually fill these from the lowest numbered slot upwards, but your motherboard's manual will tell you exactly what to do. Once you know which slot you're using, press on the plastic catches at each end so they pivot fully open. Line up the notches on the module with the slot, then insert it by pressing down at both ends. The two catches should clip over the ends of the module as it moves down into the slot. If there's a lot of resistance, check again that it's lined up properly.

4 **FINISH OFF** Add any further memory in the same way. Check that the catches are properly engaged in each occupied slot, then replace any components you removed, close the case and reconnect everything. When you switch back on, watch the POST (power-on self-test) and check that the amount of memory shown matches the total you expect. Here it's 1048576K, which equals one gigabyte.

HOW LONG?
Having sourced your RAM, installing it should only take 15 minutes.

HOW HARD?
If you have the right RAM, you shouldn't have any problems.

TIP

If you want to make sure your new memory is working properly, visit www.memtest.org/#downiso to download the Memtest86+ utility, choosing the appropriate version for your system.

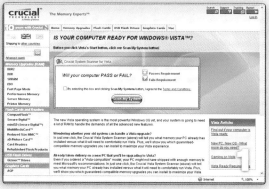

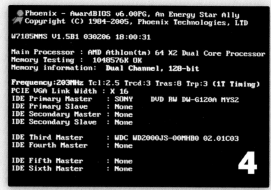

HOW LONG?
Two hours to fit; allow
another two if it's your
boot disk.

HOW HARD?
If you've never done
it before, follow the
instructions carefully.

TIP

▶ If you do bend a pin
on your hard disk's
data connector, it may
be possible to fix it.
Try teasing it back
into place with a small
screwdriver – but be
very, very gentle.

HOW TO...
UPGRADE YOUR PC'S HARD DISK

*Even if your PC meets Vista's minimum requirements – a 20GB drive with
15GB of free space – there are plenty of reasons to upgrade your hard disk,
not least the low price and high capacity of modern drives.*

1 **SATA OR PATA?** If your PC's motherboard
has a SATA connector – which is possible if it
was bought in the last two years; check your
manual – then add a SATA hard disk as shown here.
They're neater, due to the slimmer cables, and easier to
configure. However, for this guide we'll assume you're
installing a Parallel ATA hard disk, often called an IDE
drive, as this is the more common format in older PCs.
A 250GB disk costs around £60, and our tests have
shown the Hitachi Deskstar T7K250 to be suitable for
recording TV and fast backups. It's also quiet. Most
7,200rpm Parallel ATA drives should also be fine.

2 **IDE CONTROLLERS** If you're installing a Parallel
ATA drive, you should be able to plug it directly
into one of the motherboard's IDE controllers.
Most motherboards have two, and each can have up to
two devices attached using a ribbon cable with three
plugs (if two-plug cables have been used, you'll need
to replace these to get two devices per controller). The
existing hard disk will be on the primary controller, with
the CD and/or DVD drive on the secondary. Fitting a
hard disk on the same IDE controller as a CD or DVD
will work, but reduce the disk's performance.

3 **MASTER AND SLAVE** If you install two hard
disks on the same IDE channel (using the
same ribbon), you should set one as a master
and the other as a slave. This is done using jumpers:
clips that you slide onto pins found on the back of
the drive. It's best done before you slide the hard disks
into position in the case, especially as every drive will
have a guide to its jumper settings printed on it. If
you're going to be installing Vista straight away, make
sure your new disk is also in the Master position on the
cable, and that your old disk is set to either Slave or
Auto via its jumper.

4 **CONNECT THE DRIVE** Screw your hard disk
into position and connect its power plug.
Before attaching the IDE cable, notice that
the connectors only fit one way. Don't force them: if
you bend the pins on a drive's IDE connector, it may
be beyond repair. Note that if you install an empty drive
as the primary master, your PC won't boot; you should
only do this if you're going to install Vista now. If, once
installed, Windows doesn't report the full capacity of
the disk, you may need to flash the BIOS. Follow your
motherboard instructions closely to avoid damage.

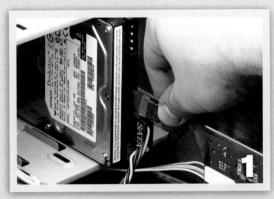

IN THIS CHAPTER

26 **How to... Back up your data in Windows XP**
It's vital to safeguard your files before an OS upgrade, and XP provides a simple way to do it.

30 **Step by step: Install Vista as an XP upgrade**
To preserve your PC setup, programs and files, you can install Vista as an upgrade – and it's cheaper too.

28 **Step by step: Windows Vista clean install**
Tidying your files away and replacing XP with Vista, it's the simplest install option, especially with our guide.

32 **How to... Create a dual-boot system**
XP and Vista, on the same PC – the best of both worlds. Or is it? Read our guide and avoid the pitfalls.

CHAPTER 2

GETTING GOING

You should be pleasantly surprised by the Vista install process. The ugly, intimidating text-based setup of old has been replaced by slick graphics and needs minimal intervention once you've entered your product key and decided where and how to install the OS. In this chapter, we guide you through the three ways you can install. Do a 'clean' installation, and Windows XP is

IN VISTA

swept away, to be replaced by a virgin copy of Vista. Second is the upgrade install option, an attractive proposition for those with trusty XP systems set up just the way they like. Finally, you can set up a dual-boot system, which is a little more advanced. Whichever you choose, you should back up your data in Windows XP before installing, so turn to p26 first.

HOW LONG?
Half an hour to several hours, depending on the amount of data.

HOW HARD?
Very easy: the Wizard takes you through the whole transfer process.

HOW TO...
BACK UP DATA IN WINDOWS XP

Whether upgrading to Vista or installing afresh, you'll have existing files you don't want to lose. Windows XP's Files and Settings Transfer Wizard is compatible with Vista to a certain extent, and provides a simple way to transfer your data.

1 START THE WIZARD Within Windows XP, go to Start, All Programs, Accessories, System Tools and click on the Files and Settings Transfer Wizard to begin the process. The Welcome window will prompt you to close any other applications that are running, and you should certainly do this to ensure nothing interferes with the process in any way. After clicking Next to continue, you're asked if this is your new or old computer. Select Old Computer to let the utility know that this is the PC with your existing files on it.

2 CHOOSE STORAGE LOCATION You'll need some form of external storage to house the files during the transfer. Even if you opt to install Vista as a direct upgrade from XP, which should retain your personal files, it's still wise to carry out this procedure for added security. If you only plan to transfer a small quantity of files, you may be able to fit them onto a CD, DVD or USB flash drive, but it's more likely that you've built up a large amount of data over the years. The best option is a second hard disk, either inside your PC or an external drive connected using USB or FireWire. If your PC is connected to a network,

you can use another computer or a network attached storage (NAS) device to store your data temporarily. The Browse button can be used to direct the wizard in the right direction.

3 CHOOSE FILES OR SETTINGS Although the next window gives you the option to back up application settings, this isn't compatible with the Vista restore utility which you'll be using later, so you should choose to back up your files only. The pane on the right contains a list of everything that's currently selected for backup; if you would like more control over what's saved – and this is recommended – tick the box at the bottom left before continuing.

4 SAVE YOUR VITAL DATA Your currently selected folders are on the left, and you can use the buttons on the right to remove any of them and add others. You'll need to navigate your way around the basic file tree to find the data you'd like to keep, so it's a good idea to have all your files somewhere simple, like the My Documents folder. The wizard also searches your entire hard disk for files of the types specified in the bottom section of the left-hand

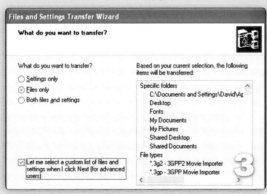

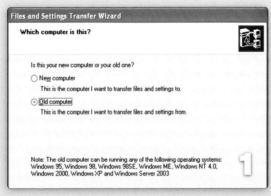

pane. If all the files you need to keep are in the folders you've chosen, it's a good idea to run down this list and remove all of the file types, thus ensuring you don't end up transferring a whole host of files you don't want or need. On the other hand, if you don't know exactly where your files are kept but, for example, want to save your entire music collection – that is, every music file on your system, regardless of where it's stored – then you could populate the list with the common audio file types. This way, the wizard will scour your PC for all files of the specified types, and add them to the backup without you having to locate them manually.

5 START THE TRANSFER You're now ready to begin saving your data, so click OK and start the process. It may take a considerable length of time to complete – quite possibly hours rather than minutes, depending on the amount of data involved – but you can leave your computer to get on with it by itself. Once the process is complete, you may be shown the details of any files that weren't backed up successfully, in which case you should manually copy those files to your backup location.

You've now completed the necessary steps to save the data from your old system. If you haven't already installed Vista, follow the steps shown over the page (depending on which type of installation you choose), then return to step 6 when you're ready to restore the files to your new system.

6 START EASY TRANSFER In Windows Vista, go to Start, All Programs, Accessories, System Tools and click on Windows Easy Transfer. This is Vista's equivalent to the Files and Settings Transfer

Wizard in Windows XP, and it's sufficiently backwards-compatible to recognise files stored by the XP wizard. Click through the Welcome window and you'll be asked whether you want to start a new transfer or continue a transfer already in progress. Choose the Continue option to let the utility know you've already backed up the files you need.

7 SELECT YOUR FILES When asked if your computers are connected to a network, tell the program you copied your files to a CD, DVD or other removable media (unless you did in fact back up your data over a network, of course). Choose the relevant storage type from the list, and you'll be asked where your backed-up files were stored. Use the Browse button to navigate to the correct location, but before your backup file will be visible (its filetype is .DAT) you'll need to use the drop-down menu in the bottom right corner to tell the program to look for files created by the Files and Settings Transfer Wizard in Windows XP. If you don't do this, it will only look for Vista's Easy Transfer files, which are stored in a different format, and your backup data won't show up.

8 RESTORE YOUR DATA The final step is simply to set Easy Transfer running. The utility will unpack all the saved files from your backup into one folder, which can then be found at C:\OldFiles. Again, this may take anywhere from ten minutes to over an hour, depending on the amount of data that needs restoring. Once the process is complete, open C:\OldFiles and you'll see your files ready to use just as before. Don't forget to copy back any extra files you backed up manually in step 5.

TIP

▶ The compatibility problems between Vista's Easy Transfer and XP's Files and Settings Transfer Wizard can be circumvented if you have access to a PC with Vista already installed. Run Windows Easy Transfer on that PC, then start a new transfer and follow the instructions to prepare your old PC. This will effectively install Easy Transfer on a CD, DVD or USB flash drive, which you can take back to your old PC and use to run the Vista utility in Windows XP. The process is then very similar to the Files and Settings Transfer Wizard, but you'll now be able to save your email, application settings and even user accounts, as well as all your important files.

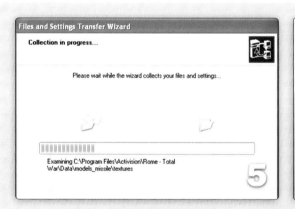

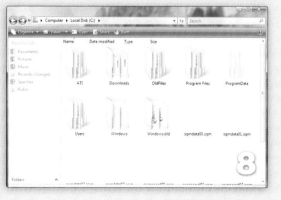

STEP BY STEP
WINDOWS VISTA CLEAN INSTALL

There are three ways to install Vista on your system, depending on whether you want to replace your existing version of Windows or keep the option of running either OS. Here's how to do a clean install, which tidies your old files away.

HOW LONG?

1-2 hours, depending on your PC's speed and how much data it holds.

HOW HARD?

Very easy – the interface is entirely graphics-based and truly intuitive.

1 **FIRST STEPS** If you've had experience of installing Windows XP or previous Microsoft operating systems, you should find the Vista install process a pleasant change. The ugly and potentially intimidating text-based setup has been replaced by slick graphics and needs minimal intervention once you've entered your product key and decided where and how to install the OS. This really is a simple enough task for any computer-literate user.

Insert the Vista installation DVD and restart the computer. You'll see a message saying 'Press any key to boot from CD or DVD'; hit a key to start the process. (If you don't see this screen, you'll need to access your computer's BIOS and ensure that it's set to boot from the DVD-ROM drive before any other drive, such as the hard disk.) You should soon see the initial setup screen, where you can alter the regional setting to the UK.

2 **ENTER PRODUCT KEY** After a couple more clicks you'll reach the product key screen, where you'll need to enter your 25-digit code. More importantly, you'll notice a checkbox marked 'Automatically activate Windows when I'm online".

It's vital to uncheck this if you're not installing your copy of Vista to its final destination – for instance, if you're testing it on a spare PC. If you uncheck the box, the installation will last for 30 days before it needs to be activated, and your key will remain unused. If you leave it checked, Vista will activate itself, and you may not be able to use the product key again.

3 **BEGIN THE INSTALLATION** After the product key screen, you'll come to the standard licence agreement screen. Tick the checkbox to indicate you accept the terms, otherwise you won't be able to continue. Next, you'll see this screen. If you'd started the install process from within Windows XP, the Upgrade option would be available (see p30). As it is, the only option is 'Custom (Advanced)'. Click this to begin the clean install.

4 **CHOOSE YOUR DESTINATION** Now to the crux of the matter: where to install Vista. You'll see a display of all your local hard disks and partitions. It may vary from the picture here, according to how many hard disk drives you have installed in your computer and how they're partitioned, but for

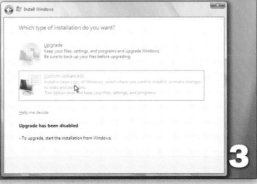

most standard PCs with a Windows XP installation it'll be more or less the same. The disk partition we've highlighted is the main system partition, containing our existing Windows XP installation. There's plenty of space free on our system, with 96.6GB available. You'll need at least 15GB free for a practical installation of Vista. Once you're absolutely sure you've selected the correct partition, click on it and then click Next.

5 PRESERVE OLD FILES If you are indeed performing a clean install on a hard disk containing an existing Windows XP installation, you'll now get this message. The Vista installation process creates a Windows.old folder and dumps your existing Windows XP installation wholesale into that. This means that all the files on your hard disk will remain intact (but remember to back them up anyway for safety's sake – see p26), so you'll be able to get to any existing documents from within Vista once it's installed. But while all your program files will also remain intact inside this folder, they won't be registered with Vista and won't appear on Vista's Start menu, so you won't be able to run them. Instead, you'll have to reinstall any that you want to use from within Vista once the installation process has completed.

6 MAKE A CUP OF TEA Once you've selected the install partition and clicked Next, the installation process begins. According to our tests, you can expect this phase to last around 40 minutes to an hour for a typical PC made within the last couple of years or so. The good news is that you can leave the installation unattended until then. When the process of copying and installing is complete, you'll just

need to set a couple of things such as a password (as we'll see next), and then your brand new Windows Vista system will be ready to roll.

7 SET A PASSWORD Nearly done. You now need to choose a username, password and, if you like, a picture to be associated with your username. If there'll be more than one user on the PC – for instance, you and your children – it can be handy to use a picture to identify the user at a glance. If you want your user account to be as secure as possible, remember not to use an obvious word as your password (see p42 for more on this): for example, the name of a pet or your own nickname wouldn't be very hard for others around you to guess. You can also enter a password hint: if you forget the password, this will be displayed as an aide memoire, but remember everyone will be able to see it, so again it should be suitably obscure to ensure it won't give a clue to anyone except yourself.

8 AUTOMATIC UPDATES The penultimate step is to decide which level of automatic updates you want. The natural choice is simply to hit Use Recommended Settings. This means that basically all the recommended online updates that Microsoft releases for Vista in the future will be downloaded and installed on your system automatically (assuming you have an active internet connection). This includes any critical security patches that may be needed if vulnerabilities are discovered in Vista. If you later find the level of automatic download activity annoys you, you can always change this setting, but initially it's better to be safe than sorry. After this step, all you need to do is confirm your time zone and you're finished.

Q What's the best way to install Windows Vista on my PC?

A There are three ways to install: you can upgrade an existing Windows XP installation, do a clean install, or you can partition your hard disk and set up a dual-boot system to let you choose which operating system you want to run each time you start your PC.

'Clean install' is the name given to the process of installing Vista onto a PC that may already have an installation of another Windows operating system – most obviously Windows XP. A clean install doesn't keep any of the settings or programs of the previously installed operating system, but it won't delete anything. It sweeps the old files away into a separate area that you'll still be able to access once the Vista installation has completed.

To see how to upgrade a system, turn over to the next page.

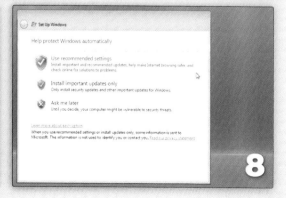

HOW TO...
CREATE A DUAL-BOOT SYSTEM

If you have incompatible legacy applications that you want to keep using, a dual-boot system – retaining your previous version of Windows – might be the best option. It's a little more complex than Vista's other installation methods, though.

HOW LONG?

An hour or so, plus several hours to back up your data first.

HOW HARD?

Be sure you're confident with the concepts of hard disk partitioning.

To set up a dual-boot system, keeping your existing Windows XP installation and running Vista alongside it, you'll need to make some fundamental changes to your hard disk's structure, creating separate partitions to hold the two operating systems independently of each other. This needn't be a particularly scary or complicated task, but it does carry a real risk of losing all the data that's currently on the hard disk, so you'll need to understand the process and prepare for it correctly. For obvious reasons, that includes backing up all your data before you even think about repartitioning.

You can deal with most of the changes required from within the Windows Vista installation process, but there's one step you need to complete before starting this. To create a new hard disk partition, you must first clear an unpartitioned gap on your hard disk large enough to accommodate it. To allow this, two conditions must be fulfilled. First, you need enough free space on your main system disk (usually C:), and second, you need software that can resize the partition on that disk. The Vista install routine can take care of creating the new partition once this free, unpartitioned space has been made available.

Before you begin the process of altering the partitions on your hard disk, you really do need to back up everything that's stored on it. We promise we're not just saying this to be cautious: some people will advise you to back up before making even minor changes to your PC, like installing a new application, but here you're looking at a completely different degree of risk. Altering partitions is something that can't be undone or reversed, and if, for instance, there's a power failure at a critical moment, all your files will be gone forever. So if you haven't done it already, turn to p26 now and find out how to back up. Until you're absolutely sure all your data is safely copied somewhere else, don't go any further with this.

To determine if you have enough free space in your Windows XP system to add Vista, double-click on My Computer, right click on your C: drive and select Properties, which will show a breakdown of your free space. Ideally you'll need at least 20GB of free space on the drive, so that you can resize the partition to leave 15GB free, giving your existing XP partition 5GB of breathing space. Of course, if you have large amounts of data that you want to keep on the disk, you may need more space than this.

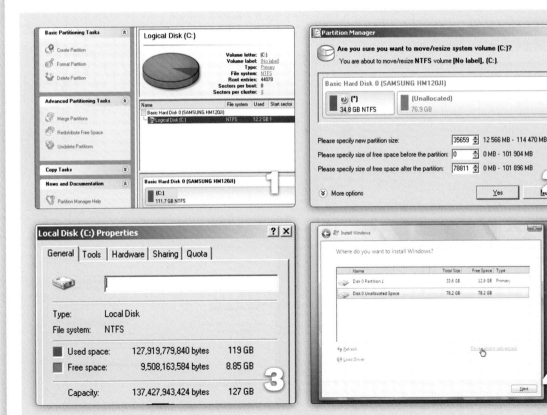

Assuming you have enough free space, you then need to get hold of software that can resize the existing C: drive. There are dozens of packages around that will do this; we used Paragon's Partition Manager 8 Personal (www.partition-manager.com), which you can download for a reasonable £26.

1 PREPARE TO PARTITION With Partition Manager, the first step is to click on the partition you want to resize. Make absolutely sure you're choosing the correct disk drive – in almost all cases, this will be the C: drive. If you have external hard disks, disconnect them first to prevent any possibility of choosing them by mistake, particularly if they contain your backups. It sounds § stupid, but we've done it.

2 RESIZE THE XP INSTALLATION Then all you need to do is click the Resize Partition icon. You can drag the right-hand edge of the existing partition to the left to free up new, unpartitioned space. Double and triple-check that you're happy with the adjustments, then click Apply. You'll need to reboot for Partition Manager (or any other partitioning software you might use) to apply the changes.

3 FREE SPACE With the existing Windows XP partition resized, your XP installation should be completely unaffected, aside from having less free space on the system drive to play with.

4 START THE VISTA INSTALL Now that you've resized your hard disk, you can proceed with Vista installation in the same way as with a clean install (see p28). Insert your DVD-ROM in the

drive, reboot the PC and hit a key to boot into the Vista install. Follow the steps on pages 28-29 until you get to the "Where do you want to install Windows?" screen. Click "Drive options (advanced)" at the bottom right.

5 SELECT A PARTITION After you've clicked on the advanced drive options, new buttons will appear at the bottom of the screen allowing you to delete selected partitions, format or create a new one. You want to create a new one, so make sure you click on the unallocated space and then click New.

6 PICK A SIZE Choose a size for the new partition in the text area that appears. By default, the value is the whole of the available free space on the disk, which is likely what you want. If not, you can reduce it. The size is shown in megabytes, not gigabytes: 1,024MB is equal to 1GB. Remember the recommended minimum free space for a Vista installation is 8GB (around 8,192MB), but you'll need at least 15GB for a practical installation.

7 INSTALL AS NORMAL The installation should now proceed in exactly the same way as a normal clean install of Vista (again, refer to p28), with a few reboots on the way and the same screens asking for your Desktop preferences, passwords, timezone and so on.

8 THE BOOT SCREEN Once the installation is finished, whenever you reboot your PC you'll get a startup options screen that will enable you to select either your old Windows XP installation or the new Windows Vista system.

Q How much hard disk space do I really need to free up for Windows Vista?

A Microsoft recommends at least 8GB free hard disk space for a Vista installation. In our tests, a clean install of Vista Home Basic took 7.02GB, while a clean install of Vista Ultimate Edition required an extra 900MB, bringing this up to 7.92GB. But remember this is simply the disk space required to install Vista itself, without taking into account the space you'll need for applications, documents, files, photos, games and anything else you plan to use. We'd consider 15GB the absolute minimum amount of free space required to install Vista as a dual-boot option and get any practical use from it.

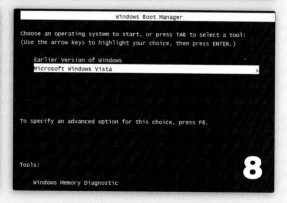

Award Winning Technology. Award Winning Service.
UK based. The clear choice.

EVERY ITEM **FREE DELIVERY**

Best PC Service & Reliability
Voted by the readers of PC Pro magazine

The Uk's Best Laptop Service & Support
Voted no.1 two years running by readers of What Laptop magazine

To celebrate the launch of Windows Vista™

Low price Core 2 Duo

19"

DUAL CORE

NOW with 19" TFT screen

SAVE £50

Solar XS
£499 inc VAT (£424.68 ex VAT)

- Intel Pentium D processor 820 (2.8GHz, 2x1MB cache, 533MHz)
- Genuine Windows Vista™ Home Basic
- Direct 2D/3D graphics (on board)
- 19" flat panel TFT display
- 512MB DDR 2 RAM 667MHz
- 160GB Serial ATA 7200rpm hard drive with 8MB buffer
- Multi Format Dual Layer DVD Writer (18x) / CD-RW (40x) drive
- On-board 6 channel audio
- Mini tower case (352x180x365mm) 4xUSB2.0 & 10/100 LAN
- Logitech keyboard & optical wheel mouse
- Bronze 1 year warranty

RECOMMENDED UPGRADE > £100

- Intel® Core™2 Duo Processor E4300 (1.8GHz, 2MB cache, 800MHz)
- Genuine Windows Vista™ Home Premium
- 1GB DDR 2 RAM 667MHz (2x512MB)
- 250GB 7200rpm hard drive with 8MB buffer

Double Memory NOW 1GB

---

18 months 0% finance

Pay monthly. 18 months 0% finance. 10% deposit. From £19.95 per month. 18 equal monthly instalments.

18 MONTHS 0% FINANCE

Solar Base 5000
£699 inc VAT (£594.89 ex VAT)

- Intel® Core™2 Duo Processor E6400 (2.13GHz, 2MB cache, 1066MHz)
- Genuine Windows Vista™ Home Premium
- 256MB NVIDIA GeForce 7600 graphics with TV-out & DVI
- 1GB DDR 2 RAM 667MHz (2x512MB)
- 320GB Serial ATA 7200rpm hard drive with 8MB buffer
- Multi Format Dual Layer DVD Writer (18x)/CD-RW (40x) drive
- On-board audio
- Mini tower case (352x180x365mm) 4xUSB2.0 & 10/100 LAN
- Logitech Internet Pro cordless keyboard and mouse
- Bronze 1 year warranty

RECOMMENDED UPGRADE > £300

- Intel® Core™2 Duo Processor E6600 (2.4GHz, 4MB cache, 1066MHz)
- Genuine Windows Vista™ Ultimate
- 256MB NVIDIA GeForce 7900GS graphics with TV-out & DVI
- DVD-ROM (16x) drive in addition to multi format drive
- Midi tower case (453x222x495mm)

"The most powerful computer you're likely to get for £799"
Computer Active Issue 230

19"

Computer Active BUY IT!

Solar MX100
£799 inc VAT (£680.00 ex VAT)

- Intel® Core™2 Duo Processor E6300 (1.86GHz, 2MB cache, 1066MHz)
- Genuine Windows Vista™ Home Premium
- 256MB NVIDIA 7600 graphics with TV-out & DVI
- 19" widescreen flat panel TFT display with built-in speakers
- 1GB DDR2 RAM 533MHz (2x512MB)
- 320GB Serial ATA hard drive with 8MB buffer
- Multi Format Dual Layer DVD Writer (18x) / CD-RW (40x) drive
- Hybrid TV tuner card, receiver and remote control, supports analogue/digital
- On-board audio
- Creative I-Trigue 3220 2.1 speakers
- Mini tower case (352x180x365mm) 4xUSB2.0 & 10/100/1000 LAN
- Logitech Internet Pro cordless keyboard and mouse
- Optional floppy drive & modem
- Silver 3 year warranty

CALL OR VISIT OUR WEBSITE FOR MORE GREAT VALUE PRODUCTS INCLUDING HIGH DEFINITION

FREE Software Included on all PCs

Microsoft Works 8
Word processor, spreadsheet and database applications

BullGuard Internet Security
Anti-virus with *FREE* 90 day updates - plus firewall & online backup

Roxio Easy Media Creator 7
CD/DVD creation, video editing and DVD playback software

Bronze 1 YEAR WARRANTY
1 year return-to-base service (parts & labour). National rate telephone support

Gold 3 YEAR WARRANTY
1st & 2nd year in-home service (parts & labour). 3rd year return-to-base (parts & labour). National rate telephone support

Silver 3 YEAR WARRANTY
1 year in-home service (parts & labour). 2nd & 3rd year return-to-base (labour). National rate telephone support

Platinum 3 YEAR WARRANTY
3 years in-home service (parts & labour). National rate telephone support

 Windows Vista™

Windows Vista™ is here.

Go online for latest pricing. Visit an Evesham store today for the true Windows Vista experience.

Don't forget your software!
Upgrade your PC to include Microsoft's stunning new Office 2007 software. Packages start from as little as £108

Visit selected stores*
Wednesdays 6 -7pm
for Vista hour

• Demonstrations
• Advice
• Competitions

BUY NOW PAY 2008[1]
On all products over £350
5% deposit

"Ultimate system that lets you have it all"

19"

Solar Ultimate GT

£1299 inc VAT (£1105.53 ex VAT)

• Intel® Core™2 Duo Processor E6600 (2.4GHz, 4MB cache, 1066MHz)
• Genuine Windows Vista™ Ultimate
• 256MB NVIDIA 7900GS graphics with TV-out & DVI
• 19" widescreen flat panel TFT display with built-in speakers
• 2GB DDR 2 RAM 667MHz (2x1GB)
• 320GB Serial ATA 7200rpm hard drive with 8MB buffer
• Multi Format Dual Layer DVD Writer (18x)/CD-RW (40x) drive
• On-board audio
• Creative I-Trigue 3220 2.1 speakers
• Cooler Master Stacker 831, 350w PSU, 6xUSB2.0 & 10/100/1000 LAN
• Logitech Internet Pro cordless keyboard and mouse
• Optional floppy drive & modem
• Gold 3 year Parts & Labour warranty

(intel) Core 2 Duo — Dual-core. Do more.)

"Fast & feature rich"
PCW, Editors Choice, Jan 07

15.4"

PCW Editors Choice JAN 07

FREE 3 YEAR WARRANTY

Voyager C530

£749 inc VAT (£637.45 ex VAT)

• Intel® Centrino™ Duo Mobile Technology: Intel® Core™ 2 Duo processor T5600(1.83GHz, 2MB cache, 667MHz)
• Genuine Windows Vista™ Home Premium
• Intel graphics
• 15.4" WXGA X-Bright wide screen display (1280x800)
• 1GB DDR2 RAM 667MHz (2x512MB)
• 100GB 5400rpm Serial ATA hard drive
• DVD/CD-RW/Dual Layer DVD-RW drive
• Wireless Mini PCIe 802.11abg (54Mbps) LAN
• 6 cell Li-Ion battery (life up to 3hrs approx)
• 4xUSB2.0, VGA, Express Card & 10/100 LAN
• Weight - 2.8kg Dimensions - 359x255x34mm
• Silver 3 year warranty

(intel) Centrino Duo — Core 2 Duo inside)

RECOMMENDED UPGRADE > **£200**

Voyager C530RD as Voyager C530 with:
• Intel® Centrino™ Duo Mobile Technology: Intel® Core™ 2 Duo processor T7200 (2GHz, 4MB cache, 667MHz)
• Genuine Windows Vista™ Home Premium
• 256MB ATI Mobility Radeon X1600 graphics

Ultimate mobile performance

17"

PC Plus Editors Choice Hotlist

What Laptop Silver Award

CustomPC PC Approved

Voyager C720DC

FREE PROCESSOR UPGRADE

£1449 inc VAT (£1233.19 ex VAT)

• Intel® Centrino™ Duo Mobile Technology Intel® Core™ 2 Duo processor T7200 (2GHz, 4MB cache, 667MHz)
• Genuine Windows Vista™ Ultimate
• 512MB NVIDIA GeForce Go 7950 GTX graphics
• 17" WSXGA X-Bright widescreen display (1680x1050)
• 1GB DDR2 RAM 667MHz (2x512MB)
• 100GB S-ATA 5400rpm hard drive
• DVD/CD-RW/Dual Layer DVD-RW drive
• Wireless Mini PCI 802.11abg (54Mbps) LAN & Bluetooth
• 1.3M Pixel camera
• Built-in media card reader (MS/Pro, MS Duo, MMC, RSMMC, SD, Mini SD)
• 8 cell Li-Ion battery (life up to 2hrs approx)
• 4xUSB2.0, Firewire, Serial, DVI, S/PDIF out, TV-out, Express Card & 10/100/1000 LAN
• Weight - 3.8kg Dimensions - 397x294x44mm
• Gold 3 year Parts & Labour warranty

(intel) Centrino Duo — Core 2 Duo inside)

LCD TVS, DIGITAL TV RECORDERS AND OTHER PERIPHERALS

(intel) Core™2 Duo inside™
Dual-core. Do more.

evesham TECHNOLOGY

Buy online
www.evesham.com
Call 0870 162 2110

Visit an Evesham store 0870 160 9800
Try Windows Vista™ for yourself

Altrincham	Birmingham*	Bristol	Cambridge
Evesham*	Glasgow*	Ipswich	London
Milton Keynes	Norwich	Nottingham*	Peterborough
Reading*	Southampton	Swansea*	Tunbridge Wells

CHAPTER **3**

WELCOME TO W

Getting used to any new operating system can be a daunting experience, and Windows Vista is no different. Although it's the friendliest version of Windows yet, it's also quite complex – each different edition comes with a wealth of features that may initially seem bewildering, but will soon become indispensible. In this chapter, we'll go through the

INDOWS VISTA

basics: how to find your way around Vista's very different user interface, how to tweak it to suit your way of working, and how to make the most of some of its new features. We'll also get to grips with how to set up your user accounts – an important concept in Vista – to give you maximum control while ensuring your system is safeguarded.

YOU COULD LEAVE YOUR WINDOWS DESKTOP AS IT COMES, BUT IT'S MORE PRODUCTIVE – NOT TO MENTION SATISFYING – TO TWEAK IT TO YOUR LIKING.

Personalising the Desktop

Windows Vista lets you change just about every aspect of its appearance. Most of the important settings for this purpose are in one place: the new Personalize section of the Control Panel. You'll find a link to the latter in the Start menu.

You can also quickly access the Personalization menu by right-clicking on the Desktop and selecting it from the menu. Alternatively, press the Windows key on your keyboard, type 'pers' and press Enter. Note that, even when Vista is set to run in UK English, 'personalisation' (with an 's') won't work.

DISPLAY RESOLUTION The first job is to ensure that you're running your screen at the right resolution. Vista will make a good guess when it's being installed, but if you're using a notebook or an old-style CRT display, there's a good chance it will need adjusting manually. CRT monitors don't have a fixed resolution, so you can experiment to see what works best for you, but flat panels are made up of a set number of pixels (check your manual for details), and should be set to this native resolution to prevent big black borders or a distorted picture.

Head over to Control Panel, Personalization, Display Settings. Move the slider at the bottom (which shows your current resolution) left or right to see all

your options. You should be able to move it all the way to the right to get your maximum resolution, then click Apply. Don't worry if your screen disappears or becomes corrupted – just don't touch anything, and it should revert back to your previous setting automatically after 15 seconds.

DESKTOP BACKGROUND The first time you load Windows Vista (unless you've bought your computer from someone who's already done this), you'll be given a choice between six Desktop background options. But Vista actually comes with lots more: 36, to be precise. These range from famous paintings and landscapes to abstract light schemes.

To browse through all these backgrounds, go to Personalization, Choose Desktop Background and you'll see them organised into themed groups. Click on one you like the look of, and you'll see the change made immediately – click Cancel if you want to go back to what you had before.

You can also use one of your own pictures as a Desktop background. Click Browse and navigate to wherever your picture is stored. This folder location will also be remembered and added to the drop-down list at the top for future reference.

These are four different ways you can make your Desktop look – the choices are virtually endless. For details on how to do it, see opposite.

TIP

▶ If you've got a notebook with a high-resolution screen, you might find icons and text on your Desktop look tiny. Reducing the resolution would compromise display quality, but there's a much better (if rather hidden) answer.

1. Go to the Control Panel (in the Start Menu) and type 'dpi' into the search box at the top-right corner. Select Adjust font size (DPI), then click continue at the confirmation prompt.

2. By default, Vista is at 96dpi – change this to 120dpi. You'll then be prompted to restart your PC before the change will take effect.

3. After a restart, the new setting means that text and icons will be bigger, but you won't lose any detail.

HOW TO...
CUSTOMISE YOUR DESKTOP

The changes you can make to your Desktop needn't be purely cosmetic. Arranging icons and the Taskbar to suit the way you work, can save time again and again. Having said that, purely cosmetic changes can be fun too…

1 **ADD ICONS** If you want to have more than just the Recycle Bin on your Desktop, you can quickly add other common shortcuts using the Start menu. From there, your User folder, Computer and Control Panel all have right-click options to Show on Desktop. You can also add more shortcuts by right-clicking any application or folder and selecting Send To, Desktop (create shortcut).

2 **CUSTOMISE THE TASKBAR** Customising the Taskbar can be a real help if you habitually run several programs at once. One of the most useful changes may be simply to increase its height. Right-click on any blank area and select 'Lock the Taskbar'. Move your mouse to the top of the Taskbar, until you see the pointer become a double-headed arrow: you can then drag it up (or down) as much as you want. We'd suggest doubling its height. That way, you get the day and date added to the clock, as well as twice as much room to manage currently open programs. You can also drag the Taskbar around so that it docks at the top or either side of your screen, but we've rarely found this useful. Once you're happy with your Taskbar's size and position, lock it again (using the same right-click menu) to prevent it being moved accidentally.

3 **QUICK ACCESS TOOLBAR** It's worth taking the time to add your favourite applications to the Quick Access toolbar, which sits just next to the Vista Start Orb. You can drag-and-drop any icon from the Start menu here (including the Computer shortcut) to get one-click access to it, as well as rearranging or deleting the existing ones. Again, you can unlock the Toolbar and resize or move it to show all the icons you want – grab the dotted grids.

4 **GO FURTHER** If you want to make more radical changes, you'll need the Appearance Settings window, which allows you to change just about every aspect of the screen furniture. Go to Personalization, Window Color and Appearance, then click on 'Open classic appearance properties for more color options'. You'll get a list of predefined looks, including the option to switch from Windows Aero (where available) to the Windows Basic or Standard themes. You'll also find the Classic theme, which will make Vista look a bit like Windows 95, as well as some high-contrast themes for visual accessibility. The Advanced button at the bottom right lets you change everything from the size of title bars to the fonts used in menus – your opportunity to make a real mess.

HOW LONG?
Allow 20 minutes. Take your time – it could save you time later.

HOW HARD?
Even the advanced options are pretty simple to master.

TIP

Once you're happy with all the changes you've made, you can save them as a Theme. Go to Personalization, Theme and use the Save As button. It won't save your Taskbar or Sidebar settings, but it's a handy way to switch quickly between different looks.

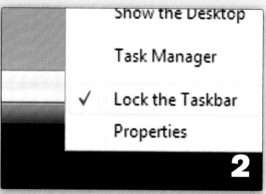

IN WINDOWS VISTA, SEARCH IS EVERYWHERE – IT'S A FUNDAMENTAL PART OF
WHAT MAKES THE NEW OPERATING SYSTEM STAND OUT FROM THE OLD.

Introducing search in Vista

Forget the clunky, slow search facility in Windows XP that trawled through your hard disk while you sat and stared at a hugely irritating cartoon puppy dog. Vista's search facilities are of a different order, and form the core of the new interface.

If you've used recent search utilities such as Google Desktop or Microsoft's own MSN Desktop Search, the concept behind Vista is similar, only far more tightly integrated into the operating system. The essential idea is that you don't bother navigating to what you want with laborious points and clicks, battling the ever-present irritation of forgetting where things are. You simply type what you're looking for into a search box. Vista maintains a continuously updated index of all your files, documents, photos, emails and programs.

A NEW WAY OF WORKING The index is lightning-fast, and you'll often find that what you're looking for has been found before you finish typing. This even extends to the Start menu: rather than clicking on the Start Orb and navigating through the menus to get to the application you're after, just hit the Windows key on your keyboard and start typing the application's name – the keyboard focus will automatically be in the search box. Once you start typing, the default list of programs (such as Welcome

Center) is replaced by programs that match the keys you just entered. You'll soon find, like us, that you don't bother with the mouse any more to start a program: hitting the Windows key, typing the first few letters and hitting Enter is so much quicker.

Beyond the basic Start menu search facility comes the new Windows Explorer interface, which has had a total revamp (see below). Again, it's now based far more on searches than navigating folders in traditional point-and-click style. The Search box in the upper-right corner is where you start, and from there you can customise and modify your searches and even save common searches in a new type of virtual folder known, appropriately enough, as a Search Folder – see p48 for more on these.

TAG IT TO BAG IT A key aspect of being able to search for non-textual content – for example, photos, music and movies – is to make sure they're tagged with meaningful keywords and relevant information. The new Explorer interface makes that easy: as soon as you click on a document or highlight several documents in a window, you'll see the metadata tags in the bottom pane. Click in one and add the relevant information. (You can give each file a star rating, too.) Although it can be a lot of effort, adding tags will make searches much more effective.

TIP

▶ Although the Search box in the upper-right corner is a ubiquitous feature of most of Vista's interface, its function varies. In Explorer windows, it's a universal tool to search the whole system. In other windows – for instance, Control Panel – it's context-sensitive: entering search terms will only give results relevant to Control Panel. It's an inconsistency, but one that doesn't take long to master.

The **Search text box** is a constant feature of Vista's interface, although it doesn't always perform exactly the same function (see Tip, far left).

Vista's **document folders** are similar to the ones you're used to in Windows XP.

You can save your own **customised searches** – see p48 for details.

Tagging your data is an integral part of Vista, and allows you to search on whole categories of files or pick out a specific one almost immediately. Each file can also have a star rating.

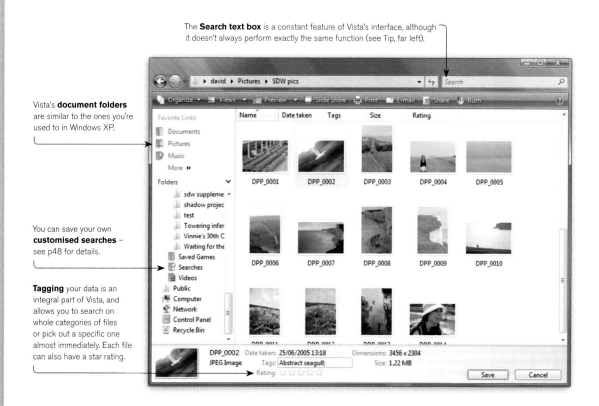

HOW TO...
GET TO GRIPS WITH VISTA SEARCH

You can carry on using Windows in the old way if you like, pointing and clicking your way around. But it's far more convenient in the long run if you train yourself to use the keyboard as first resort, and simply type what you're looking for.

The mouse was originally designed to be a more convenient option for navigating onscreen computer interfaces than the keyboard, but thanks to the power of the search engine in Vista, things are starting to come full circle and the keyboard is king once more. This is particularly true in a world where we're all storing thousands of documents and files in hundreds of folders – these days, the easiest way to find that photo or Word document is to look for keywords, in exactly the same way that we search the internet with Google. Probably the best introduction to the keyboard-based way of working is to train yourself to type the names of programs you want to run rather than clicking around for them.

1 **START HERE** Hit the Windows key on your keyboard or click the Start Orb. You'll notice the Start menu search box at the bottom of the window: the cursor is already active inside it, ready for you to start typing.

2 **TYPE YOUR KEYWORD** You can use the new Search box to launch programs as well as find files. For instance, to open Control Panel, simply start typing 'control'. After the first few letters, Control Panel will appear at the top of the list. This is an

intelligent searching tool too. Even if the word you've typed doesn't appear right at the beginning of the file name or program name you're looking for, the most relevant programs and documents will appear at the top of the list. For example, typing 'media' will bring up Windows Media Center.

3 **EASY AS ENTER** The most likely search hit is highlighted by default, so all you now have to do is hit the Enter key and the highlighted program will launch. The system is set up so that searches initiated from the Start menu here will favour program names, even though they also display other matching files. So if you happen to have a document containing the word 'control' in its title, it will be the Control Panel program that's highlighted first, and pressing Enter will open the Windows Control Panel.

4 **ADVANCED SEARCHES** The Start menu Search box can also be your launch point for more advanced document searches. If a document you're looking for doesn't immediately appear in the list, click 'See all results' at the bottom: this will launch a full Explorer search window (see p48 for more about this).

HOW LONG?
About one second!
Vista's searching is
highly efficient.

HOW HARD?
Super easy.

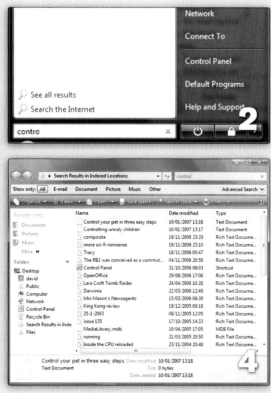

VISTA'S NEW AERO INTERFACE ISN'T JUST DECORATIVE: IT BRINGS SOME HANDY
NEW FEATURES THAT CAN MAKE A GENUINE DIFFERENCE TO HOW YOU WORK.

Introducing the Aero experience

Finding out which window is which gets much easier with Windows Flip: each icon shows a faithful miniature of the window it represents.

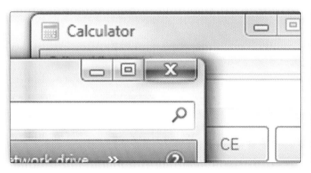

Subtle lighting effects make it clear what you're about to click on.

Hover over buttons in the Taskbar to see what they're up to.

TIP

▶ The Aero effects aren't available in Vista Home Basic Edition, so you'll have to upgrade (see p12) or live without them. You'll also need a graphics card that's fast enough (see Tip, opposite page) to get the benefit. If you meet these requirements and still can't see the effects, use Step 4 (opposite page) to check that the Aero theme is enabled. If you haven't yet installed Vista, the easiest way to find out whether Aero will run on your system is to use the Vista Upgrade Advisor: see p12 for a step-by-step guide.

Previous versions of Windows have used the computer's processor, also known as the central processing unit (CPU), to calculate what's shown on the screen. Every time you open a program or move a window, a whole flurry of instructions would be processed – potentially competing with other operations. If you've ever dragged something around the screen and seen it leaving trails, it's because the CPU is struggling to keep up.

But over the last few years, graphics cards (also known as the graphics processing unit, or GPU) have become vastly more powerful – sometimes more powerful than the average CPU. Now, Vista can take advantage of otherwise wasted power to use some subtle (and not so subtle) visual effects previously only seen in 3D games.

AERO GLASS This is the most obvious effect, with the borders of folder and program windows taking on a frosted-glass look. It's also adopted by the Taskbar (at the bottom of the screen) and the Start menu. Anything behind the glass can still be seen, with successive layers becoming grainier. Once you've got a couple of windows open, this makes everything feel less crowded and can help you focus on what you're doing rather than the window furniture.

LIGHTING & ANIMATIONS More subtle lighting effects are employed by some of the window furniture. Hover your mouse over the Close box, for example, and you'll see a 'glow' fading in, with the light reflecting off other nearby surfaces. Move away and it fades out smoothly. You'll find the same effect on various buttons. Again, hardly

earth-shattering, but in combination with the transparency effects it's pleasing enough. Windows also now sweep smoothly to and from the Taskbar, fading out as they go.

WINDOWS FLIP & FLIP 3D Pressing the Alt and Tab keys simultaneously in Windows XP presents you with a box of icons representing each of your open windows. But it's not always easy to tell which is which. Vista's Flip is much more useful, showing previews of what each window looks like. Impressively, it carries on showing any animation or video that's playing. More extravagant is Flip 3D, which tilts all your open windows into a 3D stack when you press the Windows key and Tab. You can shuffle this with the mouse wheel or cursor arrow keys to flip through to the screen you want. Both Flip and Flip 3D include a blank Desktop option – a quick way of minimising open windows to the Taskbar.

LIVE PREVIEWS It can be tricky to identify minimised buttons on the Taskbar. Enter live previews: hover your mouse over a button and (as with Flip) it will pop up with a thumbnail image of whatever's happening inside – particularly handy for quickly checking on a file operation or seeing which document is which at a glance.

ICON PREVIEWS If you've used the Thumbnail folder view in Windows XP, you'll appreciate how useful it is. Vista's Desktop and Explorer windows show most items as little versions of themselves – pictures and videos will show up as thumbnails and, if you've got Microsoft Office 2007, so will documents, slide shows and spreadsheets.

HOW TO...
CHANGE TRANSPARENCY EFFECTS

You don't have to stick with Aero's default options for transparency effects. You can switch them off, make windows more transparent, or make them more solid. Play around with the settings to find the ones that suit you best.

1 **FIND THE GLASS OPTIONS** The glass effect is the only element of Aero that you can configure in much detail, but there's a huge amount of scope to get it just as you want. You can also switch it off completely, leaving the same solid-bordered windows as in Windows XP. The quickest way of getting to the options for Aero glass is to select the link to the Control Panel in the Start menu. Then, in Control Panel's Search box at the top right, type 'glass'. The first option that appears should be 'Enable or disable transparent glass on windows'.

2 **CHANGE PROPERTIES** This takes you to the Window Color and Appearance properties. Along the top, you'll see a range of preset styles. As you click on each one, all the window borders – as well as the Taskbar – will take on a coloured hue. The slider below alters the strength of the colour tint (the default 'clear' style actually has a blue tinge). Feel free to fiddle with these, as any changes you make will be undone if you hit the Cancel button or click one of the other preset options. The option for disabling transparency altogether is also found here – just clear the checkbox. The tints will work whether glass is enabled or not.

3 **EDIT COLOURS** As if that isn't enough, there's a drop-down arrow to display a colour mixer. From here, you can adjust the hue, saturation and brightness of your colour tint, so you can match it to whatever you'd like – your football team's colours, perhaps, or something to go with your front room. Again, your changes will affect window borders, the Taskbar and the Start menu, regardless of whether or not transparency is enabled.

4 **GO CLASSIC** If you want to switch away from the Aero theme altogether, click the link labelled 'Open classic appearance properties for more color options'. This opens up a window very similar to the equivalent option in Windows XP, but with new 'theme' options. Of these, Windows Aero (where available – see Tip, opposite page) is at the top, with Windows Vista Basic, Windows Standard and Windows Classic below, followed by a number of high-visibility options that are included to aid accessibility for users with visual impairments. Classic and Standard ape the look of Windows 95 and 98, and are only really included for the benefit of anyone who simply can't cope with an interface change. If you want to switch off all the swish effects, go for Vista Basic.

HOW LONG?
Around half an hour of experimentation to get things set up just right.

HOW HARD?
Once you get used to Vista, sophisticated changes are easy.

TIP

To render the Aero effects, your graphics card needs to pass a certain performance threshold. It must also have at least 128MB of RAM onboard (or have access to your computer's main memory), and be recent enough to support the DirectX 9-level effects that Aero uses. Unless you're running something like a very low-powered notebook, the vast majority of computers from the last two years will be able to cope, as will almost any new PC you buy now.

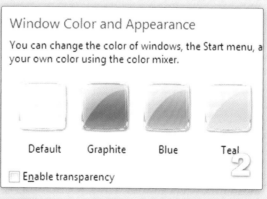

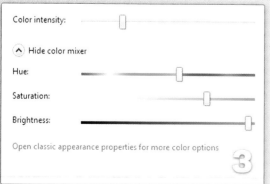

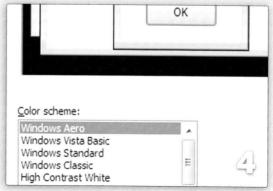

HOW LONG?
A few minutes to get to grips with the concepts, longer to master them.

HOW HARD?
It can be tough to get your head round all the options, but persevere.

HOW TO...
MASTER ADVANCED SEARCH

For almost all everyday uses, you don't need to know or think about how Vista's search engine works. But more advanced users might want to tweak search settings or search for files in unusual places. Here's how.

Once you've started to use Vista, you'll probably be very surprised at the speed at which it comes back with its search results. It manages to be so efficient because it maintains a highly optimised index of the contents of your hard disk, which is constantly updated. It doesn't just index filenames, either: it can look inside your text-based documents and index their contents too, and it takes note of the tags you apply to your photos, music and any other tagged file (see p44).

While Vista's search system is undoubtedly better than the old Windows XP method of finding things, there are one or two points you should bear in mind once you've got used to the basics and want to perform more advanced searches. First, Vista doesn't index your entire hard disk: it prioritises the more likely locations of a file you'll be searching for, namely the root of your 'User' folder, which contains folders including your Documents, Pictures, and Favorites. But if you want to search for something that may be elsewhere on your system, you have several options.

1 BEYOND INSTANT SEARCH If your search results don't yield what you're looking for first time, click on the Advanced Search entry at

the bottom of the list of search hits (or if you started from the Start menu search, click See all results, then click Advanced Search). This will produce the Advanced Search options bar at the top of the window. Advanced Search, like the search facility in XP, allows you to find files according to properties such as the date they were last modified and their approximate size. Added to that is the new ability to enter data tags and the author of a document.

2 ADD LOCATIONS To search in locations other than those that are indexed, click the bar next to the Location label at the top of the window. You can then choose a standard location, such as 'Local Hard Drives', or select 'Choose search locations…' to navigate to a particular place or folder. Make sure you click the checkbox labelled 'Include non-indexed, hidden and system files'.

3 ADD CATEGORIES Annoyingly, you can't immediately instruct the default search box to search the whole contents of files, but only their names, tags and author, which you can enter in the boxes at the top right. If you think one of those categories will

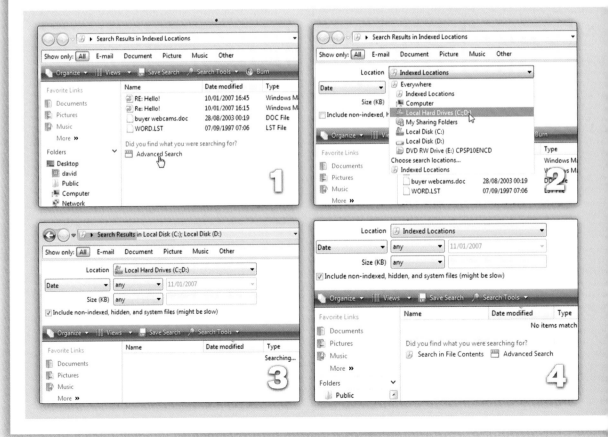

find what you want, enter some text in the relevant box. Otherwise, just hit Search. The system will start trawling the location you've specified, with the green animated bar at the top of the window showing that the search is still in progress.

4 **TOTAL SEARCH** After a while, if there aren't very many hits on your search terms, a new option will appear in the search results window, allowing you to search within files' contents. If you've had no luck so far, click it to start a comprehensive search that looks for your specified text inside documents as well as in file and folder names. Because of the limited speed of any hard disk and the amount of data that Vista now has to trawl through, opening and closing potentially thousands of files and reading their contents, the search could take some time.

5 **ADVANCED LOCATIONS** You should also notice another pop-up prompt, which will ask you if you want to take the second route to finding non-indexed documents: adding the locations of your choice to the indexing search locations. As you might expect, this will even further reduce the speed of your current search, which is why it isn't done automatically, but if you regularly want to find files in non-standard locations, this is the way to go.

6 **MODIFY INDEXING** Click on the prompt and you'll see two options: Add to Index and Modify Index Locations. Add to Index is the quick way if you just want to add the current location, but to set up indexing more comprehensively, click on Modify index locations. This will produce the Indexing Options window.

(If you're getting the hang of Vista's searching, you'll guess that you can also get to this by entering 'indexing options' as a Start menu search and then hitting Enter.)

7 **MODIFY LOCATIONS** In the Indexing Options window, click Modify and you'll see the list of locations currently set to be indexed. You'll probably be surprised that it only contains 'Offline files'. Of course, that's not really all that Vista is indexing: to see the full list, you'll need to click the Show all locations button. Once you've done that, you'll see your local hard disks in the list. Expand the C: drive by clicking on it, and you'll see that the Users folder is ticked – this includes your Documents and other standard folders.

8 **ADD EXTENSIONS** To add more locations, just navigate your way through the folder hierarchy and click the checkbox for any folders you want indexed. By default, when you tick a folder, all its subfolders are marked for indexing too. If that isn't what you want, you'll need to go through the list and manually uncheck the ones you don't want.

You should also bear in mind that the indexing engine doesn't automatically index every type of file: this is again set by a user-modifiable list. To see which file types are indexed, go back to the initial Indexing Options box and click Advanced, then click the File Types tab in the Advanced Options window. If a file type you want indexed isn't there, you can add it by typing the relevant file extension and hitting the 'Add new extension' button. Note also that you can control whether the content of a file is indexed or only its Properties (file name, size and so on) by clicking the appropriate checkbox.

TIP

▶ Although the indexed-search system is very convenient, remember that for Vista to find the file you're looking for it has to be given time to index it. If you copy a lot of files over to your PC at once, that could take hours. To quickly see whether the system is still indexing the new files, hit the Start button, type 'indexing options' in the Instant Search box and hit Enter. At the top of the Indexing Options dialog box, you'll see whether or not the index is currently complete.

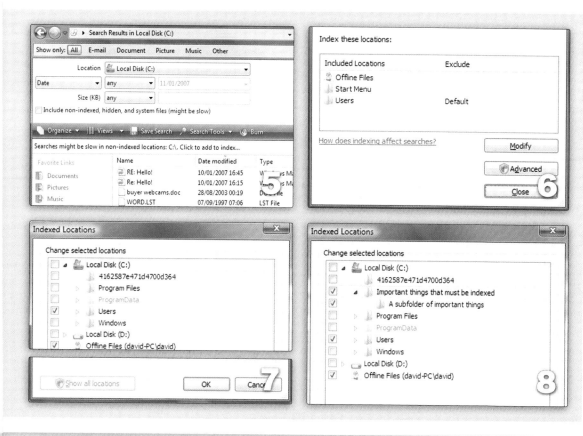

HOW LONG?
Setting up your Feed Headlines should only take a few minutes.

HOW HARD?
Once you understand how the Gadget works, it's straightforward.

FAQ

Q What is RSS?

A There's some debate about what it stands for, but Really Simple Syndication is one interpretation. It's a technology to alert people to updated news stories (and other web items, such as blog entries) on their favourite sites. You subscribe to an RSS 'feed', and whenever your chosen website is updated you'll see a new headline in your RSS reader. Click on it, and you'll either see a summary of the story or be taken straight there.

HOW TO...
SET UP FEED HEADLINES

Feed Headlines is probably our favourite Gadget, and – along with the clock and weather guide – is installed in the Sidebar by default. The Gadget isn't very intuitive at first, but this quick guide shows how to set up your favourite feeds.

1 DEFAULT FEEDS The Feed Headlines Gadget is pre-loaded into the Sidebar as standard, but if it isn't there for some reason it's simple to find: just press the + symbol at the top of the Sidebar, and Feed Headlines is one of the 11 Gadgets on offer. However, you'll soon discover that the default feeds are all from Microsoft websites – not much use if you want the most up-to-date, unbiased news. If you hover your mouse over the Gadget, you'll see a small spanner, which launches its setup screen. Somewhat counter-intuitively, though, you can't manually add a feed to the Gadget via this screen. In fact, the Gadget only displays feeds already set up in Internet Explorer, so your first task is to populate the web browser with your favoured sites.

2 ADD A FEED To add new feeds, launch Internet Explorer and head for one of your favourite sites. If it supports RSS feeds, the normally greyed-out RSS icon in the title bar (next to the Home icon) will turn orange. Many websites, especially blogs, now support RSS from their home page, but some more complicated sites require you go to their news section – in PC Pro's case, for example, go to www.pcpro.co.uk/news. Click on the RSS icon, and you'll be taken to another page where you're invited to subscribe to the RSS feed.

3 DISPLAY THE FEED Once you've added the RSS feed, click back into the Feed Headlines Gadget and then on the aforementioned spanner. You'll be offered the chance to select any combination of the feeds set up. Once you've decided which feeds you'd like to display, you can control how many headlines it displays: 10, 20, 40 or 100.

4 THE END RESULT After deciding these details, close the setup screen and you'll see all the latest news items appear in the Feed Headlines Gadget. Click on a headline you're interested in, and a larger screen will appear that includes the full headline and a brief summary of the story (plus the source of the story itself). Click on the headline, and Internet Explorer – or another web browser, if you've installed a different one and set it as your default browser – will load up the correct page. Once you've set up your feeds to your satisfaction, it's a very useful way to see all the latest stories on your favourite websites without going to the trouble of logging on to them at regular intervals.

Get the Vista™ Premium Experience....

Microsoft Vista™ Premium Certified Graphic Solutions from SAPPHIRE

SAPPHIRE X1050
Vista™ Premium Graphics Card

SAPPHIRE X1550
Vista™ Premium Graphics Card

Windows Vista™

ATI Radeon™ GRAPHICS

ebuyer
novatech
OcUK OVERCLOCKERS UK
dabs.com
SCAN
CCL
MD

SAPPHIRE
www.sapphiretech.com

IN THIS CHAPTER

56 **At a glance: Windows Explorer**
It's the main window into your system, and it looks completely different. We show you around.

59 **At a glance: user folders**
No more My Documents. Now you get a whole home folder for your files, settings and media.

58 **At a glance: the Start menu**
In Windows XP it grew like a baobab tree to eclipse your Desktop. Come and see how Vista has tamed it.

60 **At a glance: Control Panel**
Neatly categorised and with some intriguing new options, the new Control Panel is a welcome change.

CHAPTER **4**

THE VISTA DIFFE

If you need an executive summary of the major new features and user interface changes in Vista, start here. Across the next few pages you'll find a visual guide to the all-important Windows Explorer interface and those other staples of everyday Windows life, the Start menu, the user folders and the trusty old Control Panel. The designers of Vista's interface have trodden

RENCE

a fine line between familiarity and innovation, and if
you want to get the best from Vista, not get lost in it,
it will pay to study the screenshots – particularly those
of Windows Explorer, over the page. A quick read
of our annotations will reveal some of the subtleties
behind the ways in which the new features and
menus can help streamline everyday computing.

Vista's Address Bar provides a 'breadcrumb trail': click any of the locations within the current path to jump straight to that folder. Clicking on the single arrow takes you to a list of other folders in the same directory. It's a really fast way of getting around. To see a traditional file path (as in XP), click the folder icon.

Click the arrow for a list of recent folders and common locations. (If the current path doesn't fit the space, a double back arrow is shown.)

Context-sensitive **common tasks** buttons give quick access to actions you may want to perform, depending on what type of files are in the current folder. Organize and View are always there to let you customise how your files and folders are shown. Use Organize to toggle the various panes on or off.

Click on any of the **column headers** to sort by that criterion. An up arrow indicates ascending order, down means descending. Some column headers also feature a drop-down arrow that you can use to further sort, filter or categorise files.

Favorite Links is one of Windows Explorer's most useful new features. You can drag and drop folders (as seen here) into this area, and they'll be available in every Explorer window.

You can slide the **Folders** pane into view for an alternative way of navigating, similar to the 'tree' view of older Windows versions.

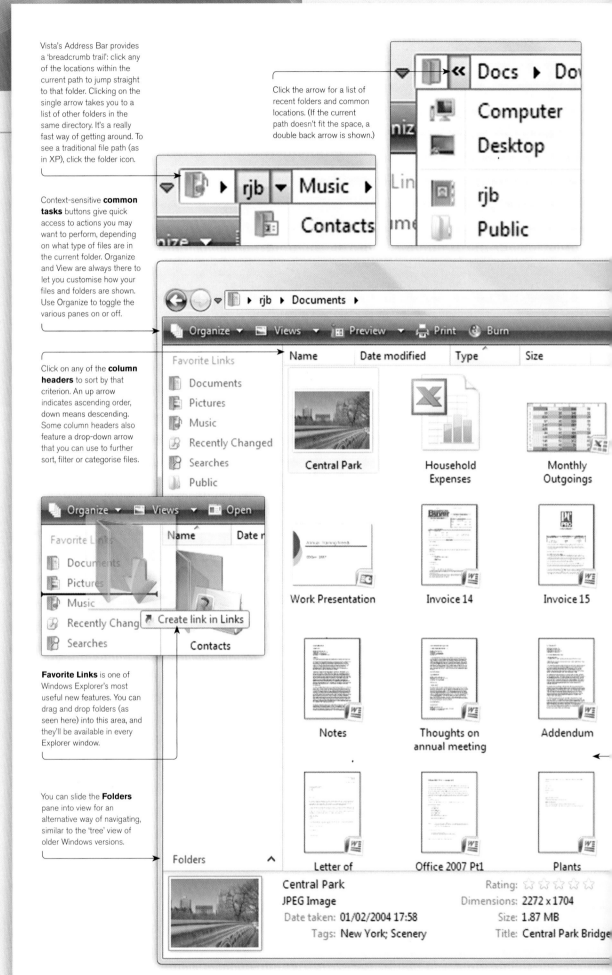

At a glance: Windows Explorer

Few areas of Windows have been so dramatically overhauled as the Explorer. Since this is the principal way to navigate your PC, there's potential for some real confusion. But most of Vista's changes are for the better, and you'll soon master the subtleties. Explorer windows are broken up into areas and panes, some of which are optional, so you won't see all of them in every window. Here's a look around the new furniture.

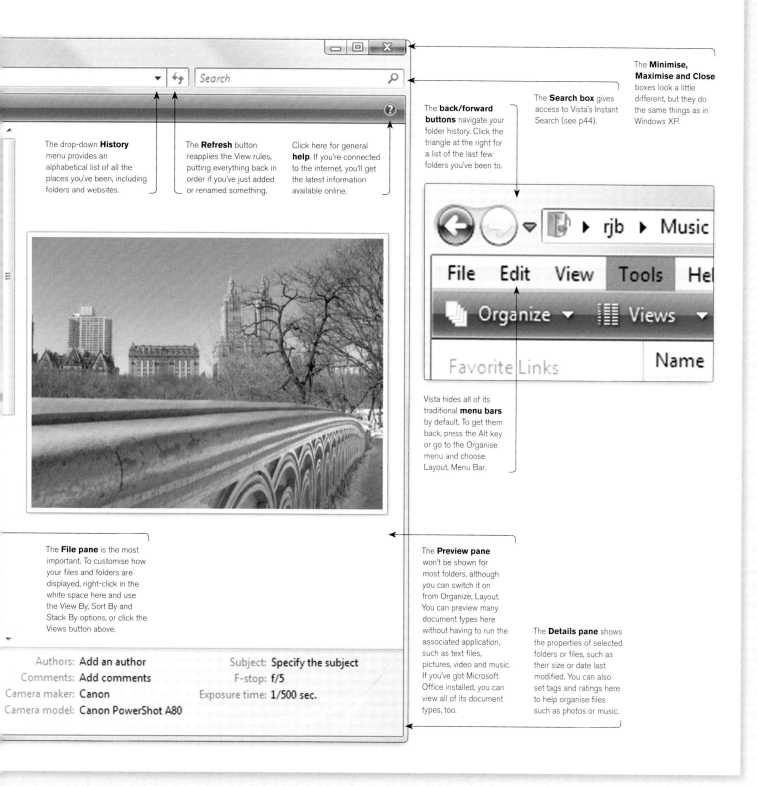

The drop-down **History** menu provides an alphabetical list of all the places you've been, including folders and websites.

The **Refresh** button reapplies the View rules, putting everything back in order if you've just added or renamed something.

Click here for general **help**. If you're connected to the internet, you'll get the latest information available online.

The **back/forward buttons** navigate your folder history. Click the triangle at the right for a list of the last few folders you've been to.

The **Search box** gives access to Vista's Instant Search (see p44).

The **Minimise, Maximise and Close** boxes look a little different, but they do the same things as in Windows XP.

Vista hides all of its traditional **menu bars** by default. To get them back, press the Alt key or go to the Organise menu and choose Layout, Menu Bar.

The **File pane** is the most important. To customise how your files and folders are displayed, right-click in the white space here and use the View By, Sort By and Stack By options, or click the Views button above.

The **Preview pane** won't be shown for most folders, although you can switch it on from Organize, Layout. You can preview many document types here without having to run the associated application, such as text files, pictures, video and music. If you've got Microsoft Office installed, you can view all of its document types, too.

The **Details pane** shows the properties of selected folders or files, such as their size or date last modified. You can also set tags and ratings here to help organise files such as photos or music.

At a glance: the Start menu

The Start menu in Windows XP was a lumbering beast. If you installed more than a couple of programs, its cascading menus soon became unwieldy, and some programs hid under several layers of folders. The good news is that it's much better in Vista. You'll also notice that the Start button has been replaced by a round button with a Windows logo, known as the Start Orb, although it does exactly the same job.

These **pinned programs**, which always appear at the top of the list, initially include only Internet Explorer and Windows Mail, but you can add your own: right-click any application icon and select Pin to Start Menu to list it here. You can click and drag the programs around to change their order.

This list of **common locations** provides shortcuts to all the most often-used places, with your user folders at the top. Uppermost is your home folder, which contains all your personal folders (see opposite page). The **Recent Items** menu shows the latest documents you've opened.

The most **recent programs** you've used will be listed here, with the latest at the bottom. You can right-click on them to pin them to the Start menu (see above) or to the Quick Launch bar.

Clicking the **user icon** is the quickest way to get to your user settings, where you can reset your password, change your picture, or manage other users of the computer.

Clicking the **power** button doesn't switch off your computer, but puts it into Sleep mode, where a trickle of power is maintained. It may not be so great for the environment, but it means your PC will power up much more quickly than from a 'cold' start (see p141). Next to it, the **padlock** icon will return the system to the log-on screen, where you'll need to enter your password to get back to the Desktop. Clicking the **arrow** button opens up a menu of less commonly needed options, including switching to another user account, logging off and restarting, as well as a full shutdown.

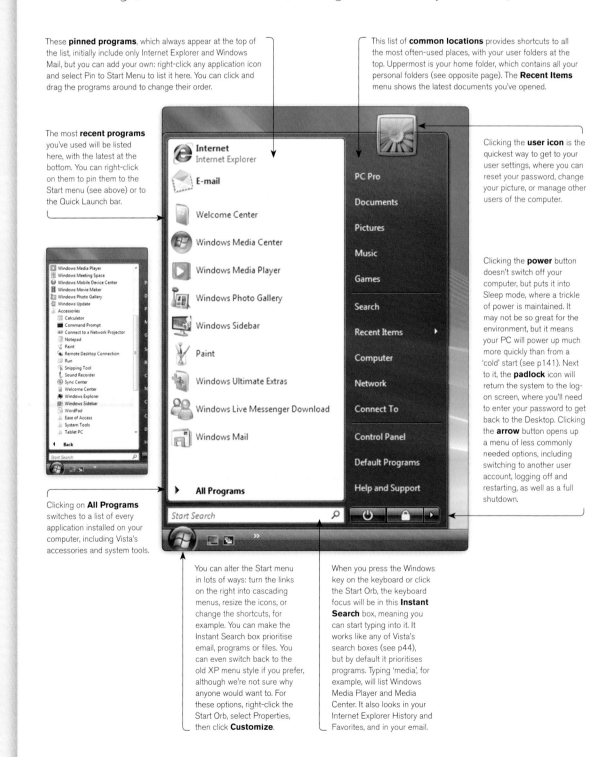

Clicking on **All Programs** switches to a list of every application installed on your computer, including Vista's accessories and system tools.

You can alter the Start menu in lots of ways: turn the links on the right into cascading menus, resize the icons, or change the shortcuts, for example. You can make the Instant Search box prioritise email, programs or files. You can even switch back to the old XP menu style if you prefer, although we're not sure why anyone would want to. For these options, right-click the Start Orb, select Properties, then click **Customize**.

When you press the Windows key on the keyboard or click the Start Orb, the keyboard focus will be in this **Instant Search** box, meaning you can start typing into it. It works like any of Vista's search boxes (see p44), but by default it prioritises programs. Typing 'media', for example, will list Windows Media Player and Media Center. It also looks in your Internet Explorer History and Favorites, and in your email.

If you prefer to keep documents on a separate drive or partition from Windows, you can **move** the locations of your user folders without losing them from your home directory. Right-click on a folder, select Properties and go to the Location tab. Click Move and browse to the directory you want to use: this could be on an external or network-attached drive. Windows will use this location from now on, but your folders are still listed in the normal way.

All the programs, files and shortcuts that exist on your Windows Desktop are actually kept in this **Desktop** folder. If you change anything here, it will be reflected on your actual Desktop.

The **Documents** folder replaces My Documents in Windows XP. This is the place to put all your everyday work files. You can add extra levels of folders within it if you want to be really organised.

Your **Contacts** folder replaces the Windows Address Book. Each contact has its own card within the folder, and there's a Gadget you can use to keep details to hand. Sadly, there's no real integration with Microsoft Outlook (if installed), and it's only loosely linked to Windows Mail.

Previously hidden away in XP, this is where Internet Explorer saves any links that you add to your **Favorites** list. Coming here (rather than using IE) is a quick route to organising them or copying them to a new computer.

The **Searches** folder houses all of your Saved Searches.

In Vista, the idea is that all games are supposed to save progress information in your **Saved Games** folder rather than hidden away in system files. There's no guarantee that developers will use it, or that older games will let you save to here, but it could come in handy in the future.

The **Downloads** folder is where Windows tries to save any files you download from the internet. You don't have to put them here, but it's good practice. Besides helping you find them more easily, this will also be good place to start clearing up if you get low on disk space.

The **Links** folder contains the shortcuts that are shown in the Favorite Links pane of all Explorer windows (see p56). You can add, rename or delete them here.

The **Music**, **Pictures** and **Video** folders are the default locations for MP3 files, photos and video clips. Media Player, Media Center and Photo Gallery look here when building their libraries or importing from your digital camera or mobile device. If you'll use the Video folder a lot, you could come here to add a shortcut to the Favorite Links folder (it isn't on the Start menu by default). Otherwise, this is the easiest place to find it.

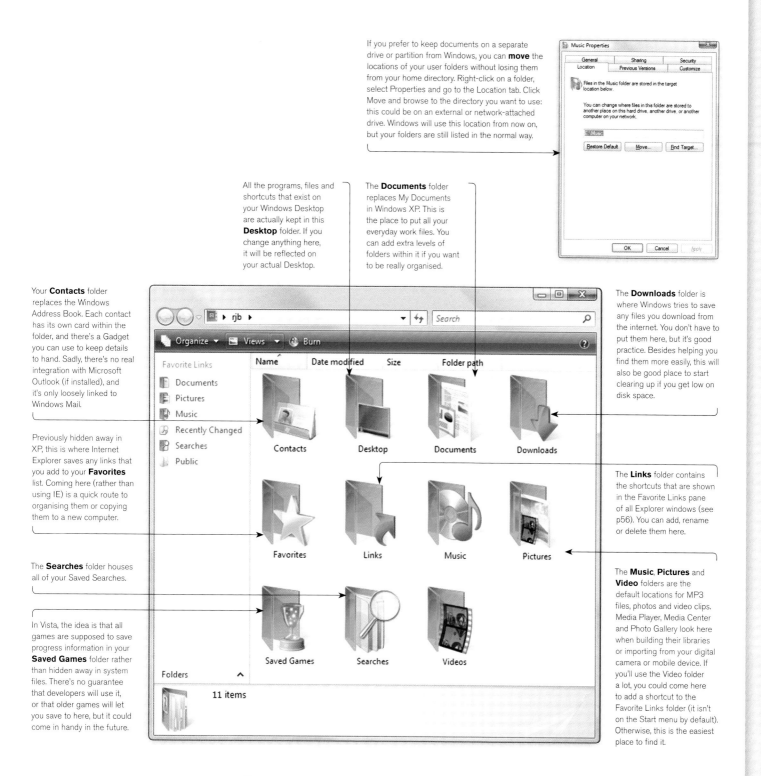

At a glance: user folders

Out goes Windows XP's My Documents, replaced by the tidier arrangement of a home folder (named after your username). This contains many of your personal settings, making them easier to back up or move to a new PC. Each user account has its own exclusive settings and documents, which you can make inaccessible to others.

Use the **Back/Forward buttons** to navigate through what you've been clicking on. Click the drop-down triangle to see where else you've been on your journey through the Control Panel.

Since Control Panel uses an Explorer window, many of the same features apply: the **breadcrumb trail** in the Address bar gives you a list of possible locations both backwards and forwards in the folder structure.

Unlike a normal Explorer window, the Control Panel's **Search box** is focused on what you can do here, rather than finding documents. Type 'desktop', for example, and you'll get a list of possible tasks you might want to perform related to the Desktop , such as changing the background or adding icons to it.

User Accounts and Family Safety provides tools for managing your user settings and parental controls, plus settings such as email and login information.

Appearance and Personalization options include Desktop background, colour scheme, Start menu, folder options, fonts and Windows Sidebar settings.

Clock, Language, and Region settings control the keyboard and date/time.

Ease of Access provides accessibility aids like high-contrast colour schemes, visualisation of audio prompts and speech control.

Choosing **Classic View** changes the list of tasks to a Windows XP-style mess of icons. It can come in handy if you want to find a specific task that you're familiar with in XP, though.

Your last few Control Panel **tasks** are listed here, in case you need to go back and tweak more.

Additional Options is for third-party apps' control panels, so it may be empty for now.

Under **System and Maintenance** you'll find 'back end' stuff like Backup, Windows Update, power management and hardware information.

Security is the home of settings for preventative

tools such as Windows Firewall and Defender. Whenever a task shows a **shield**, you'll need administrator privileges to continue.

Network and Internet options cover Internet

Explorer and any mobile devices. Infrared and Bluetooth settings are here too.

One of Control Panel's more woolly categories, **Hardware and Sound** is home

to everything from power options to printing.

The Programs section is where you manage applications (including Gadgets), set up defaults for different file types, or go online to buy more software.

TIP

▶ If you're visiting the Control Panel a lot, you could drag a shortcut to it into your Favorite Links window, or add an icon for it on your Desktop. Type the words 'icon' and 'desktop' in the Control Panel's Search box, then follow the blue 'Show or hide common icons on the Desktop' link. You can also drag and drop any of the icons from the Control Panel straight onto the Desktop.

At a glance: Control Panel

The redesign of the Control Panel in Windows Vista comes as a very welcome change from XP. The initial options are divided into ten categories, with a few common tasks below. You can click directly on these or click the category headings to get the full set of sub-categories within. If it's not immediately obvious where to find something (power settings are under Hardware and Sound, for example), try the Search bar. The easiest way to get to the Control Panel is to use the link at the bottom right of the Start menu. For a more in-depth guide, see p126.

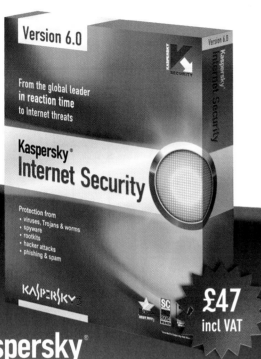

VISTA COMES WITH MICROSOFT'S NEW WEB BROWSER, INTERNET EXPLORER 7.
IT'S MORE SECURE, EASIER TO USE AND HAS USEFUL NEW FEATURES.

Introducing Internet Explorer 7

On first loading Internet Explorer 7, you may wonder where everything has gone. A clean new look hides many of the familiar options, leaving more of the screen to display web pages. Instead of a standard menu bar, a small number of icons provide drop-down lists of options. For example, pressing Home loads your chosen home page, but a triangle next to it lets you customise this setting. This means you won't have to spend time finding the right menu option. If you initially yearn for the old menu bar, it can be brought out of hiding temporarily by pressing Alt.

Some of that saved toolbar space is now used to display tabs, a new addition to Internet Explorer. With tabbed browsing, each website you open appears within the same space (rather than a separate window) but with its own named tab at the top. It's neater and lets you click quickly between sites. For a quick view of the sites you've loaded, just click on the Quick Tabs button at the top. This shows a thumbnail view of all the current web pages.

ADD-ONS If you want to search the web quickly, you no longer need third-party toolbars like those from Yahoo! or Google. Internet Explorer 7 has an integrated search bar in its own toolbar: enter a phrase to get search results from Microsoft's Live Search. Many people's first piece of customisation will be to change this to their own

choice of search engine, such as Google (see opposite page). Add-ons – small utilities that plug directly into a web browser to add extra features – are easier to manage than with previous versions of Internet Explorer. And if you want to handle RSS feeds, you don't even need extra software, because Internet Explorer 7 is more than capable of reading and displaying feeds itself.

SECURE BROWSING Internet Explorer keeps its pop-up blocker, introduced in version 6, and adds more advanced security features. Online criminals increasingly attack internet users with a technique called phishing, hoping to trick people into entering private details (such as credit card numbers) into fraudulent websites. Internet Explorer aims to highlight such sites using the built-in Phishing Filter. This warns you when you try to visit a site that's been reported as fake – we found it worked perfectly for us.

Vista users also get a new Protected Mode (not available in Internet Explorer 7 for Windows XP), which is designed to prevent software downloading or running that could be used to attack your PC. The browser also ties in with Vista's Parental Controls (see p110), and you can now delete your entire browsing history, including saved passwords and cookies, with a few clicks: go to Tools, Internet Options, General and press Delete.

TIP

▶ Printing web pages used to be hit-and-miss. Often you'd lose parts of the page off the right-hand margin and gain a blank page at the end. Internet Explorer 7 has the answer. Press the arrow next to the Print button and choose the Print Preview option. By default it's set to Shrink To Fit, which means as much of the page as possible is used and waste is reduced. If you want to override this, click the Shrink To Fit box and choose another option, such as 100%.

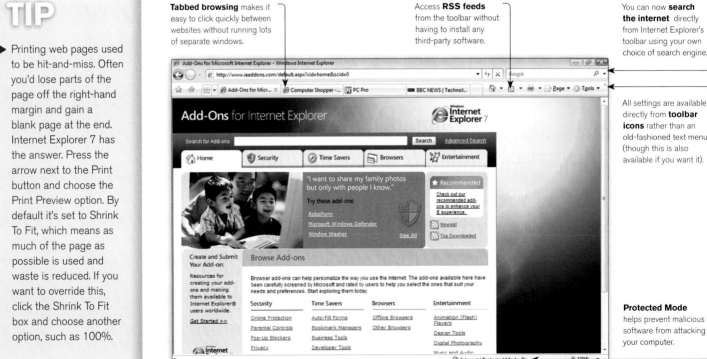

Tabbed browsing makes it easy to click quickly between websites without running lots of separate windows.

Access **RSS feeds** from the toolbar without having to install any third-party software.

You can now **search the internet** directly from Internet Explorer's toolbar using your own choice of search engine.

All settings are available directly from **toolbar icons** rather than an old-fashioned text menu (though this is also available if you want it).

Protected Mode helps prevent malicious software from attacking your computer.

HOW TO...
ADD A NEW SEARCH ENGINE

Internet Explorer 7 lets you search directly from the toolbar without any extra software. By default it works with Microsoft's Live Search, but if you prefer to use another search engine it's easy to change over to your favourite. Here's how.

1 **CHOOSE A SEARCH PROVIDER** Click on the downward-pointing triangle just to the right of the Search box in the toolbar. Choose the option to Find More Providers. This displays a list of popular search engines, including Google, Lycos and Yahoo, any of which can be used either alongside Windows Live Search or instead of it. We want to make Google our default search engine. Click on the Google icon, which is the third one down in the left-hand column. A window will pop up asking you to confirm that you want to add a new search provider. Tick the option labelled 'Make this my default search provider', then click on the Add Provider button.

2 **SWITCH YOUR SEARCH** Typing words and phrases into the Search box, or even into the main address bar, will now run a search using Google and display the results in the main window. If you don't see what you're looking for, it's simple to re-run the search using one of the alternative search engines. Don't bother visiting their websites, though. Simply click the triangle next to the Search box and choose another search engine from the list that appears. The same words and phrases will be used with this new engine and the results will appear automatically.

3 **ALTERNATIVE SEARCHES** You don't need to restrict yourself to the major search engines. Internet Explorer 7 can be set up to search lots of different databases, including Wikipedia and even Tesco. If Microsoft doesn't provide the site you want as a default option in Internet Explorer, you can always try to add it yourself. Visit the site you want to use, and try its search facility using the word 'TEST'. Make sure you use capital letters. When the results are displayed, click in the address bar and select the text (this is the address of the search results page). Press <Ctrl-C> to copy it to the Windows Clipboard.

4 **ADD A SEARCH ENGINE** From the Search tool menu, choose the Find More Providers option, as in step 1. Paste the web address you just copied into the first space in the yellow box by pressing <Ctrl-V>. Type a name for this new search site into the second box and click the Install button. The site should now be searchable directly from the toolbar.

If you change your mind later on and want to remove a site or reset the browser to use the default search engine, click the triangle again and choose Change Search Defaults. Select a site and choose Set Default or click Remove.

HOW LONG?
Less than 10 minutes, once you decide where you want to search.

HOW HARD?
Easy, as long as your chosen sites return queries in the toolbar.

TIP

▶ Remember, Internet Explorer isn't the only web browser you can use. Mozilla Firefox 2, from www.mozilla.org, works very well with Vista, and many people prefer to use it simply because they feel it's more secure than any Microsoft browser. Online criminals are more likely to attack Internet Explorer than Mozilla, which has far fewer users and therefore fewer potential victims.

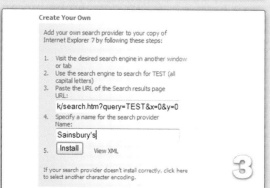

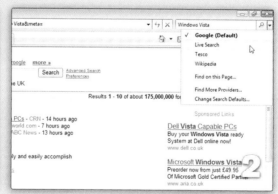

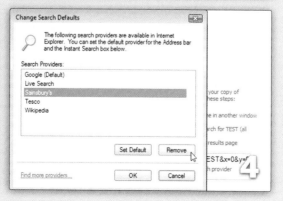

HOW LONG?
Around half an hour, depending on what settings you tweak.

HOW HARD?
Read our advice first, but you don't need specialist knowledge.

HOW TO...
SURF THE INTERNET SAFELY

Internet Explorer 7 in Windows Vista brings extended security features to help you use the internet while minimising the likelihood of your PC being attacked by viruses, scams or spyware. Here's our guide to setting it all up successfully.

1 SECURITY ZONES Click on the Tools button and choose Internet Options. Click the Security tab to view the different security zones. These allow you to customise security settings according to what sites you visit and where they're located. For example, you can have one set of options for web servers on your own local network, another for general websites on the internet and yet another for internet sites that you trust. Click on the Internet icon near the top and check that the slider below it is set to at least Medium-high. This should ensure that malicious websites are blocked. Also check that the Enable Protected Mode option has been ticked, so even if some nasty program slips through, it won't be able to run properly.

2 TRUSTED SITES Sometimes you'll want to lower your defences for certain sites so that security restrictions don't hamper their operation, perhaps for your online bank or a web-based email service. Click the Trusted sites icon and move the slider to your preferred level of security. The default setting of Medium is a sensible choice. You now need to create a list of sites to which these more relaxed security rules apply. Click the Sites button and type in the web

addresses of your trusted sites. If you've already visited them, their addresses will appear as you type the first few characters. There's a setting at the bottom labelled 'Require server verification (https:) for all sites in this zone'. By default it's turned on, which is fine if all of your trusted sites use encryption. If they don't, you'll get a warning and will need to untick this before you can enter the sites' details.

3 THIRD-PARTY COOKIES Although cookies aren't as much of a security problem as some people believe, it's still useful to be able to block some sites from being able to set them. Click the Privacy tab to view the general settings for your internet zone. The default settings are a good compromise, letting you use sites that require cookies while blocking third-party cookies. Third-party cookies aren't set by the site you visited, but by an affiliate, usually an advertising company that's providing the site's adverts. Blocking them won't cause you any harm and will prevent these marketing companies from tracking your use of the web. Make sure the "Turn on Pop-up Blocker" option is also set to prevent annoying adverts that create their own windows; these may also attempt to set cookies.

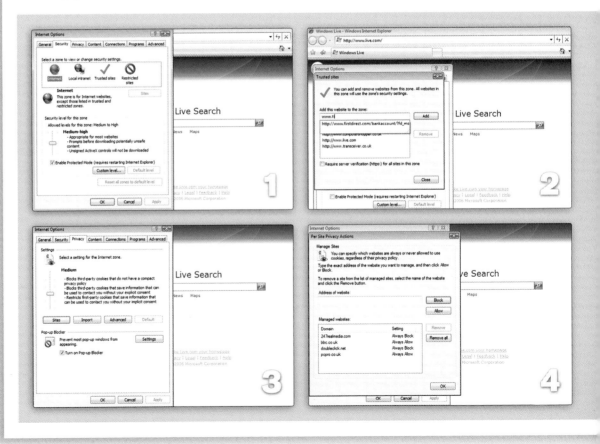

4 **MORE COOKIES** Occasionally you may want to override the general Cookies settings, allowing some sites to set cookies under any condition and blocking others completely. Click on the Sites button and type the addresses of these sites, adding them to the list with the Block or Allow button. If you make a mistake, just select the entry and click the Remove button.

5 **CONTENT ADVISOR** Not only can Internet Explorer 7 protect you from hackers and other security problems, but it can also prevent you and other users of your PC from accessing unsuitable material online. Click the Content tab to gain access to the Parental Controls and the Content Advisor. If you don't use different user accounts for everyone who uses your computer (see p42), the Content Advisor is a simple way to choose what kind of sites can be visited. You must set a password so that only you can log in to change the settings. But this option is much more limited than using separate accounts with Parental Controls (see p110). The most useful security setting in this window is the AutoComplete button. Click it to see a list of entries, including options to save data entered in forms and usernames and passwords on forms. Untick all of these for maximum privacy and security.

6 **COVER YOUR TRACKS** If you've been using AutoComplete up to now, you should erase the form data and passwords it's saved. Click the General tab or choose Delete Browsing History from the Tools menu icon. You can clear out temporary internet files, cookies, history, form data and passwords all in one place. Press Delete all to get rid of the lot. If you've followed the previous steps, you'll rarely need to do this again.

MORE SECURITY EXTRAS

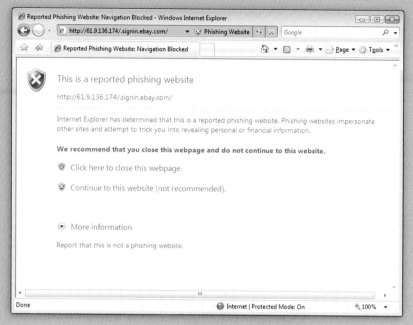

The new **Phishing Filter** built into Internet Explorer 7 sits quietly in the background, checking each site you visit against a predefined list. When you visit a suspicious site, you'll receive a warning. Initially the filter uses a list of sites that Microsoft stored on your PC when Internet Explorer was installed. When you first launch IE7, you'll be asked if you want to enable automatic checking. If you do, the filter will sometimes send web addresses that you visit to Microsoft so they can be compared against a list of reported phishing sites. Even if you don't want to enable the automatic check, you can still use the system manually. When you visit a suspicious site, click on the Tools menu icon and choose the Phishing Filter option. Then click Check this website.

When you visit an online shop or use a web-based email system, your username and password should be encrypted, or others could intercept and use them. In previous versions of Internet Explorer, **encrypted connections** were indicated using a small yellow padlock in the status bar. Now it's more obvious because the padlock is larger and appears in the address bar. Clicking on it displays information about the site, including verification that it's run by the correct organisation and isn't a fake. For more details of the site's digital certificate, click on the View certificates link.

Some sites publish their **privacy policies** in an electronic format. This is so that Internet Explorer (and other browsers) can tell automatically whether or not the sites claim to keep to themselves any information they collect about you. Internet Explorer can use this information to decide whether or not to allow the site to set cookies. If you want to read these policies yourself, visit the site you want to check out, click Internet Explorer's Page menu icon and choose Web Page Privacy Policy. The existence of a privacy policy isn't a guarantee that the site will do what it claims, however.

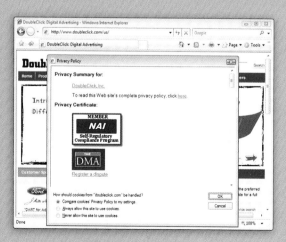

HOW TO...
SHARE AN INTERNET CONNECTION

If you have a broadband internet connection, it makes sense to share it between all your computers so they can use it simultaneously. You can do this quite easily using a wired or wireless router. We'll look at the wired option first.

HOW LONG?
2-3 hours, depending on your knowledge of networking.

HOW HARD?
Can be fiddly, but many routers have wizards to make setup easier.

1 **CONNECT THE ROUTER** If your internet connection is via ADSL (the most common form of broadband, using conventional phone lines) then it makes sense to buy a router with a built-in ADSL modem; this will replace any existing modem provided by your broadband supplier, which probably connected to your PC via USB. Check with your broadband supplier for compatible routers, as it should have a list of recommended products and instructions on how to set them up, although in practice other products may work fine too. If your internet connection is via cable (commonly from ntl:Telewest, now known as Virgin Media), choose a standalone wired or wireless router and connect your existing cable modem to the router port marked WAN.

2 **CONNECT A COMPUTER** Connect your first PC to the router using a standard network (Ethernet) cable, which may come with the router. A window will pop up in Vista asking what type of network it is, with three options: Home, Work or Public. Choose the appropriate one, bearing in mind that you'll need to be logged onto your PC with an administrator account (see p42) to select Home or Work.

3 **ENTER SETTINGS** Next, enter your internet connection settings into your router. You'll manage your router with a configuration utility that displays as a web page. Your router's manual should tell you the web address to access this: for example, http://192.168.2.1. Open Internet Explorer and enter this into the address bar at the top. Your router's web interface should appear. You may have to enter a username and password (given in the manual) either now or when you make changes. Many routers have wizards that take you through entering your details, but you'll need information such as your broadband username, password and type of connection (PPPoA or PPPoE). If you don't know these, ask your broadband supplier.

4 **FIX PROBLEMS** If your router's interface didn't appear when you typed in its address, it could be because the DHCP server isn't enabled in the router. A DHCP server makes the connection between your PC and the router automatic, and in the vast majority of routers it's enabled by default. Vista, too, is set by default to automatically connect to a network. If you can't connect to your router, though, you may need to manually set your PC to have an address that

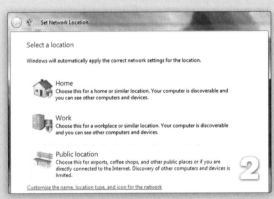

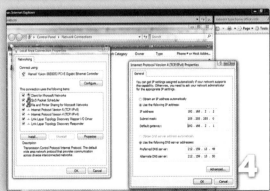

matches the router's. You needn't understand the details, just follow these steps. Right-click the Network icon on your Desktop (or in the Start menu) and select Properties. This will display the Network and Sharing Center. Click Manage Network Connections in the list on the left and you'll see one or more icons. Right-click the one called Local Area Connection and select Properties. Double-click the Internet Protocol Version 4 list entry and you'll see a window where "Obtain an IP address automatically" is selected. Select "Use the following IP address" and type your router's address into the Default gateway box: for example, 192.168.2.1. Type 255.255.255.0 into the Subnet mask box, then type 192.168.2.2 into the IP address box. (You can choose anything between 1 and 255 for the last number, as long as it doesn't clash with the Default gateway address.) Click OK in each window until you're back at the Network and Sharing Center.

5 ENABLE DHCP SERVER If you had to use step 4, type your router's IP address into Internet Explorer's address bar to check that you can now get its web interface. Once you can, it's worth enabling the DHCP server to make future connections automatic. If you can't immediately see where the DHCP server options are, check your router's manual, but it should be a simple case of clicking a radio button.

6 TRY IT OUT To find out if your settings have worked, type a website's address into Internet Explorer and hit Enter. If the site appears, your router is set up. Now all you need to do is repeat step 2 for every other PC you want to share the internet connection with. Most routers provide up to four wired connections. For more on networking, see p128.

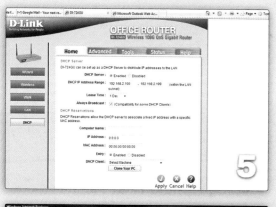

ROUTER SETUP TIPS

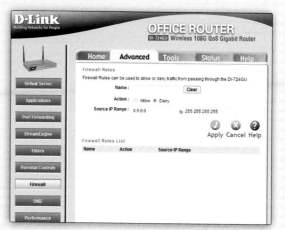

When you first browse to your router's interface, you may be slightly overwhelmed by the options. It's worth checking first that the **firewall** is enabled. A firewall can protect your computers from any harmful incoming traffic, although you should still leave Windows Firewall activated too. Unless you know what you're doing, leave advanced firewall options alone. Firewalls can also prevent outgoing traffic. If you need to allow a particular program access, look for an Applications option in your router – this is the easiest and safest way of configuring the firewall.

Most routers allow you to control access to websites, and can also restrict times when access is allowed. This is sometimes referred to as **Parental Controls**. Some routers let you create a list of disallowed sites, while others only support a list of allowed sites. Many let you create policies that schedule when and to which machines the rules should be applied. Alternatively, you might find an option to monitor which websites a particular computer is viewing. Options may be spread across different screens, so it pays to search around your router's menus (and manual).

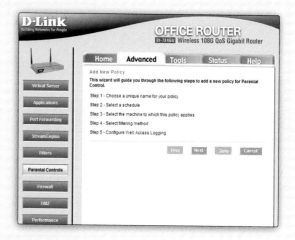

To connect computers in different rooms, a wireless network (see p70) is the obvious alternative to trailing long network cables around and drilling holes in walls. But, depending on the size and construction of your home, the location of your PCs and a variety of other factors, Wi-Fi networking may not always work for everyone. Several manufacturers offer so-called **Home Plug** devices which plug into a normal wall power socket, using the mains wiring to transmit data. You simply attach a network cable from each PC to a plug, and a connection is automatically established between them. Transfer speeds vary, with cheaper plugs providing as little as a third of the speed of the fastest, most expensive options. Due to the cost of these plugs, it's only worth investing in them if Wi-Fi isn't an option, since a wireless adapter will work out much cheaper than a pair of Home Plugs. To find out more about the Home Plug concept, visit www.homeplug.org.

HOW TO...
SHARE BROADBAND WIRELESSLY

A wireless router gives you the freedom to use the internet from anywhere in your house. With a wireless adapter fitted to each PC or notebook, it's a convenient way to make the most of your broadband connection. Here's how to set it up.

HOW LONG?
2-3 hours, depending on your knowledge of networking.

HOW HARD?
It could be a breeze, but wireless networking problems can be tricky.

TIP

▶ Place your router as high up as possible to get the best-possible coverage. Use a high shelf, or wall-mount the unit and point the antennae directly upwards. You might find this increases your wireless range up to double compared with placing it on the floor.

1 CONNECT THE ROUTER As with a wired router (see p68), if your internet connection is via ADSL you'll want a router with a built-in ADSL modem, while cable users will need a standalone router to connect to the cable modem, provided by the cable company: just plug a standard network (Ethernet) cable into the WAN port on the router. If you're unsure which router to buy, check out the recent reviews at www.pcpro.co.uk. Note that while your computers can connect to the router wirelessly, the router must be cabled to your broadband socket, so it'll need to be in the same room.

2 CONNECT A COMPUTER Most routers have Wi-Fi turned off by default, so you'll first have to connect a PC using a standard network cable. (If possible, you may want to leave your main desktop PC attached to the router with a cable rather than connecting wirelessly, as this will ensure the fastest and most reliable connection.) A window will pop up asking what type of network it is, with three options: Home, Work and Public. Choose the appropriate option, bearing in mind that you'll need to be logged onto your PC with an administrator account (see p42) in order to select Home or Work.

3 ENTER SETTINGS Next, enter your internet connection settings into your router. You'll manage your router with a configuration utility that displays as a web page. The router's manual should tell you the web address to access this: for example, http://192.168.2.1. Open Internet Explorer and enter this into the address bar at the top. Your router's web interface should appear. You may have to enter a username and password for the router (given in the manual) either now or when you make changes. You should activate password protection and set your own password as soon as possible so that Wi-Fi-equipped neighbours can't access your settings. Many routers have wizards that take you through entering your details, but you'll need information such as your broadband login and type of connection (PPPoA or PPPoE). If you don't know these, get them from your broadband supplier.

4 ENABLE WIRELESS Router interfaces can vary widely, but the wireless settings should be fairly prominent. Look for a heading such as Wireless, Wi-Fi or WLAN and you should find On/Off or Enable/Disable radio buttons. Once you've enabled wireless, click Apply or OK to activate the setting.

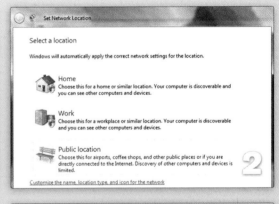
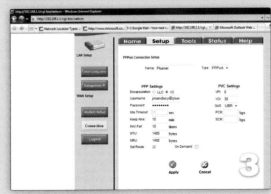
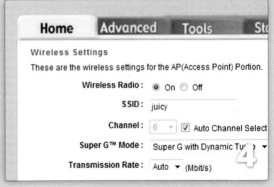

5 **ENABLE SECURITY** Although you could now try and connect to the internet using a wireless notebook or PC, you should first configure wireless security settings. If you don't, you could open yourself up to a world of trouble. Neighbours could easily (even accidentally) connect to your router and share your internet connection, and more importantly hackers could capture sensitive information, such as credit card details and your name and address, when you purchase something online. The most secure wireless mode is WPA2, but not all wireless hardware supports this. If your notebook or PC's wireless adapter doesn't, use WPA. Choose a password, making sure it's different from your SSID (see step 6). Finally, choose an encryption or cipher type, which will be TKIP, AES or both. Again, choose a setting your wireless adapters support. Stick with the default if you're unsure.

6 **CHANGE YOUR SSID** The SSID is the name of the router, which will appear when anyone in the area searches for wireless networks. If you leave it at its factory setting, it may be the same as a neighbour's router, which means you won't know which is yours when you try and connect to it – and nor will they. Choose a name you'll remember, but not one that could identify you or your house. For extra security you can tell your router not to broadcast a name at all. If you choose this option, you'll still need to remember the name so that you can type it in when connecting to the router for the first time from another computer.

7 **FIND THE NETWORK** The next step is to connect to your router using a computer with a wireless adapter. Wireless adapters are available as internal expansion cards for PCs and notebooks and also as external USB devices. Make sure the adapter is enabled: use the utility provided with it to check, and if it's in a notebook, make sure any physical switches are turned on. Some notebooks have a key combination, for example <Function-F5>, which you need to press to toggle the wireless adapter's power on and off. Once wireless capability is turned on, a 'Connect to' window should appear listing the wireless networks that have been found. If not, there are several ways to access this window in Vista: for example, by clicking Start, then Connect to, or from the Manage wireless connections dialog box.

If you have an Apple Mac computer running Mac OS X, it's just as easy to connect this to your router. Apple's built-in wireless capability is known as AirPort, and you can configure it in the Network pane of System Preferences, although your Mac should automatically detect a wireless network and offer to connect to it.

8 **CONNECT WIRELESSLY** Click on your network name – which should be marked as a Security-enabled network – and you'll then be asked to type in your password. If your network isn't listed because you chose not to broadcast the SSID, click Set up a connection or network at the bottom of the Connect to window. You'll then be able to type in your details manually, although bear in mind you'll need to have your SSID, security type (such as WPA), encryption type (such as TKIP) and password to hand. Simply save the settings and you should be securely connected, ready to access the internet without wires.

TIP

▶ Wireless routers are a confusing breed, with many different codes and acronyms to try and negotiate. You'll find the relevant terms in the glossary at the back of this guide (from p156), but most people should choose an 802.11g router for now. Although 802.11n is the fastest standard, most existing wireless cards in PCs and notebooks won't support it, so you'll only get 802.11g speeds. For this and other reasons, you may not get any practical benefit from 802.11n, and in any case an 802.11g network should already work much faster than the broadband connection you're sharing, so it won't slow down internet access.

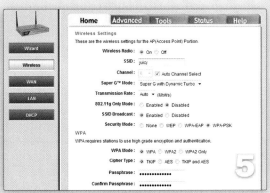

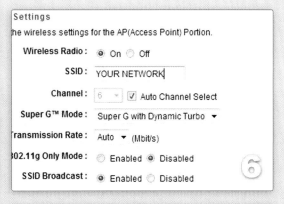

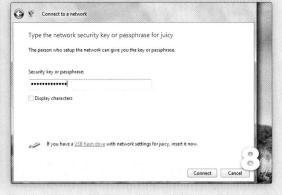

CHAPTER **6**

THE NEW BUNDL

In previous versions of Windows, it almost felt as if Microsoft's bundled applications were last-minute efforts that were there only to tick boxes rather than actually be used. With Vista, they start to take pride of place; many of the new programs are so good you'll never again consider expensive third-party software. For email, there's Windows Mail, a rejuvenated and much

ED APPS

better-equipped successor to Outlook Express. Then there's Windows Calendar, which lets you manage your appointments and share them. You can see your music as well as hear it in the all-new Windows Media Player, and interact with your digital images better than ever with Windows Photo Gallery. There's even a decent video-editing package.

VISTA COMES WITH A NEW VERSION OF THE WINDOWS MEDIA PLAYER JUKEBOX. BASED ON A MORE STREAMLINED ENGINE, IT LOOKS AS GOOD AS IT SOUNDS.

Introducing Media Player 11

TIP

▶ To use WMP 11 more discreetly, right-click anywhere on the Taskbar and go to Toolbars, Windows Media Player. Next time you minimise Media Player, instead of becoming a passive Taskbar button it'll shrink down to a mini version of its transport controls, over by the system clock. You can stop, skip or pause, adjust volume, or hover your mouse over the controls to see the artist and title plus a progress bar. Videos will even play at a tiny size.

The primary job of Windows Media Player is to handle music, and if that's all you want to do, it's ridiculously easy to use. Load it up, let it search through your music, and it's raring to go. But Windows Media Player (WMP for short) has much more to offer beneath the surface, and version 11 benefits from a certain amount of fine tuning.

The key music features can be found in the tabs along the top, allowing you to hop quickly from one function to another, while more advanced features are in the drop-down menus underneath them. Sync lets you load music onto an MP3 player, Burn is for putting your own music compilations onto CD or DVD, and Rip will extract music from your audio CDs (see opposite page).

NEW INTERFACE It's the Library and Now Playing tabs where you'll spend most of your time, with the column running down the left-hand side offering lots of different ways to browse through your music. You can view by artist, album title, song title, genre or – one of our favourites – by year. There's an old-fashioned text-based view, or, if you know your albums by their covers, you can also view them by their artwork, as seen below. Compared to previous versions you might have used, it's a visual treat, and a huge improvement from the version of Media Player that came with Windows XP.

IMPROVED PERFORMANCE WMP 11 is also much, much faster than previous versions. In our tests, we loaded it with more than 2,500 albums (the equivalent of a 15-metre-high pile of CDs) and found we could still skip through the music library with ease. Then there's the ever-present Vista Search box, which returns accurate results in less than a second. As you'll soon get used to in Vista, the search results narrow down instantly while you type, and often just a few letters will be all you need. You can search across artist, album, song or genre, and to keep you up to date there's also a new Recently Added section that will instantly find the last few albums you've put into your library – a simple but very effective time-saver.

EASIER SHARING There's integration with other media hardware and software, too, as WMP will now act as a 'server' for other devices. If you've got a wireless router for your broadband connection (see p70), you can connect a whole host of different media-streaming devices to it and access your PC's music from anywhere in the house. It's the sort of feature that would have cost you thousands of pounds a few years ago, but now comes ready to go on your computer. And, if you've got another PC or notebook on your network and it's running WMP 11, you can share your music between computers (see Tip, right).

The **Layout** and **View Options** buttons control how Media Player shows your music library.

Use the **Media Guide** to browse online stores for music or read reviews of the latest releases.

As in Windows Explorer, a **breadcrumb bar** lets you jump to where you want to be in your library.

You can quickly browse your music by any of these **categories**.

The **transport controls** include shuffle and repeat buttons. Click the arrow buttons to skip forward or back, or hold down to fast-forward or rewind. In the right corner are buttons to shrink Media Player down to the Taskbar or expand it to full-screen.

HOW TO...
RIP YOUR CD COLLECTION TO PC

Transferring your music onto your PC opens up all sorts of possibilities. Via the internet, Media Player will look up each CD in a database and download the song titles and album cover to complete the process. Here's how to start ripping.

1 OPEN THE OPTIONS Take a minute to get the settings right: the default options will leave your music sounding OK but not great, so we recommend ramping up the quality. Putting your CDs onto your PC at full, uncompressed CD audio quality would need around 650MB of storage space per album, soon filling up all but the largest hard disks, let alone MP3 players. Various compressed formats are available to use significantly less space, and if you're careful you won't notice the difference. Click under the Rip tab and go to More Options... to bring up the Rip settings.

2 SET YOUR STANDARDS Unless there's a good reason to change it, you can leave the top section alone and move down to the Rip settings. The Format drop-down menu lists a number of options, each of which has its own advantages. For the best balance of quality and disk space, we'd opt for Windows Media Audio (Variable Bit Rate). Set this at the top half of the quality scale and most people won't notice the difference from CD. This format isn't compatible with Apple iPods, however, so if you own one, or intend to in the future, it's better to play safe and choose the more universal MP3 standard. You'll need much higher bit rates (and more disk space) to keep it sounding good,

though. If you're a music lover, you might find the default 128Kb/sec (kilobits per second) quality objectionable – instead, take it up to the maximum 320Kb/sec, although that will eat up around 400MB per album.

3 ADVANCED SETTINGS If you're planning on ripping more than a couple of CDs at once, tick 'Rip CD when inserted' and 'Eject CD when ripping is complete'. You can now put the CD in. The first time you do this, you'll be prompted to add copy protection to your music. Don't do it, unless you want to restrict how you can use the files you've ripped. Click the copyright acknowledgement and then OK.

4 SIT BACK AND RELAX You should now get the Rip window. If you're connected to the internet, you should soon see the album art and song titles appear, with a progress indicator for each track next to them. If you're ripping a very obscure CD, or your own compilation, WMP may not recognise it, in which case you can go back later and edit the titles yourself. If you've ticked the appropriate option, the CD should eject when finished, and you can then put the next one in. Repeat until you're done. For a lot of CDs, this might take a few weekends, but it only needs doing once.

HOW LONG?
A few minutes to get the hang of it, then your CD collection's the limit…

HOW HARD?
Nothing to it except choosing sensible compression settings.

TIP

If you've got computers running Windows XP on the same network, you can get a version of Media Player 11 for them too. All of your computers will then be able to share music. You'll get a prompt when the PCs find each other, and you can either allow or deny each one access. If you allow it, the contents of the other computer's music library will show up in your Library view and you can use it in the same way as music stored locally.

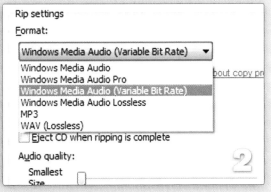

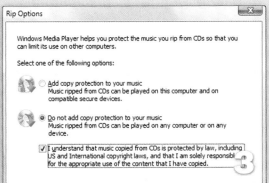

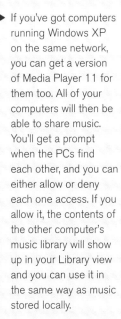

EMAIL IS ONE OF THE BEST REASONS TO BE ON THE INTERNET, AND ALL VERSIONS OF WINDOWS VISTA COME WITH A COMPLETE EMAIL CLIENT BUILT IN.

Introducing Windows Mail

Windows has handled email via the Outlook Express mail client for years, but this feature has been given a thorough overhaul in Vista. Not only does it have numerous new features, it also gets a new name. However, if you're used to either Outlook Express or its more complex cousin, Outlook (traditionally bundled with Microsoft Office), you won't have too much trouble getting to grips with Windows Mail – it's even easier to use than before.

Like much of Vista, Windows Mail looks fairly familiar, but plenty of work has been done behind the scenes. The engine that stores and handles all your email has been rewritten to make it faster and more stable, and it's now able to handle much larger archives of messages.

NO MORE JUNK One of the best new features is that Windows Mail will now deal with spam. Every message that comes in is scanned for tell-tale signs, and if Mail thinks it's spam, it's moved to the Junk E-mail folder. As the people who send spam wise up to the methods used to detect it, new rules will be sent out to Windows Mail via Windows Update, so you can always stay one step ahead of the marketers. If you find that a message you want has been classed as spam by mistake, you can designate either the sender or their whole domain (such as anyone@microsoft.com) as 'safe'. Alternatively, you can turn off the spam filter or reduce its sensitivity, or go the other way and lock everything down so that only known senders get through to your inbox.

GONE PHISHING Phishing emails are both a nuisance and dangerous. This is where spam tries to tempt you to enter personal information, such as your bank account details, into a fake web page, or take you to a site that will install unwanted software on your PC. While Vista contains a number of other features to prevent this from happening, Windows Mail offers a preventative measure in its Phishing filter: each email is scanned to make sure it doesn't take you to a website that's known to be fraudulent, or contain common phishing tactics.

INSTANT SEARCH As with so many areas of Windows, Microsoft has integrated Vista's Instant Search into Windows Mail, and it makes a big impact on usability. Search lives at the top right of Windows Mail, and narrows down the results as you type. Even if you never delete or file your email, it should now be easy to find that important ticket receipt or password reminder. As all your emails are indexed by Vista's search engine, they'll also show up in the Start menu and other Search windows, so you don't even need to be in Mail to find them.

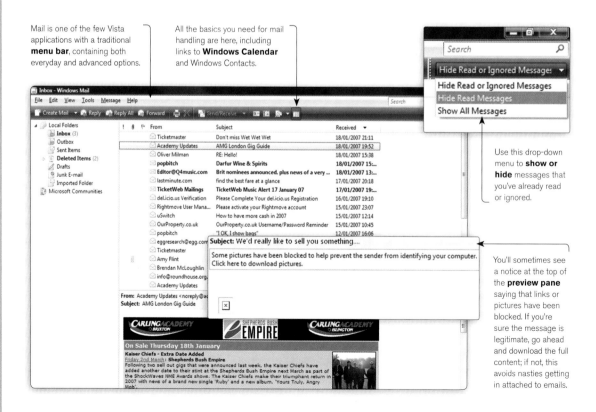

Mail is one of the few Vista applications with a traditional **menu bar**, containing both everyday and advanced options.

All the basics you need for mail handling are here, including links to **Windows Calendar** and Windows Contacts.

Use this drop-down menu to **show or hide** messages that you've already read or ignored.

You'll sometimes see a notice at the top of the **preview pane** saying that links or pictures have been blocked. If you're sure the message is legitimate, go ahead and download the full content; if not, this avoids nasties getting in attached to emails.

HOW TO...
USE RULES TO SORT YOUR MAIL

If you get more than a few emails a week, you'll soon have an unwieldy inbox. Filing important messages in separate folders can help you keep track of them more easily. Using rules, you can do this (and plenty else besides) automatically.

1 **CREATE A FOLDER** If you want to set up a general filter, such as one to put all your bank statements into one folder, first create a new folder in your inbox. Right-click on the Inbox and choose New Folder… You'll get a dialog box where you can enter a name for it. Create as many folders (or subfolders) as you need to organise your messages.

2 **ADD A NEW RULE** Now go to the Tools menu, go to Message Rules, and follow across to Mail… The New Mail Rule window has four steps: Conditions, Actions, Description and Name. In each of them, you can select from a whole range of criteria, either individually or using several at once.

3 **STATE YOUR CONDITIONS** The conditions you can set include who the message is from, who it's addressed to (you may have more than one mailbox, or you may want to filter messages with fictitious addressees) and other properties such as its size or attachments. In this case, we want to find only bank statements, not other messages from our bank, so we're specifying both who the message is from and what it's about. There are even more options for Actions: you can copy, move or forward an email, make

it show up in a specific colour (particularly handy for separating personal emails from the more mundane ones at a glance), or prevent it being downloaded from the mail server at all. In our example we want to choose the option to 'Move it to the specified folder'. As you check the boxes, you'll see the rule beginning to take shape in the Description section at the bottom of the window, with all the elements that you can edit underlined and highlighted in blue. Click on the 'Where the from line contains people' link; to specify a sender, you can either select an existing name from your Windows Contacts or create a new entry. We're going to add the email address that our bank statements come from, and add the word 'statement' to the Subject line condition, so the rule only handles messages whose subject includes this. The last step is to name your rule.

4 **APPLY YOUR RULES** Once you've clicked OK, you'll see your new rule entered into the list. Click the Apply Now button and Mail will trawl through your inbox, moving any messages you've already received that fit the conditions. Every time you receive new email in future, the rule list will be checked – in the order you've chosen – and your bank statements will be filed neatly away in the folder you selected.

HOW LONG?
About 20 minutes, and setting up rules now will save you hours later.

HOW HARD?
You don't need any great technical skills, just common sense.

TIP

▶ As well as changing the way your email is presented using the filter settings or message rules, you can rearrange Mail's windows. The most powerful way is to go to the View menu and select Layout. You can add or remove parts of the interface so that it's not cluttered with elements you don't need. On a decent-sized monitor, our favourite tweak is to move the preview pane from below to beside the message, avoiding the need to scroll down.

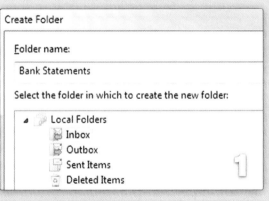

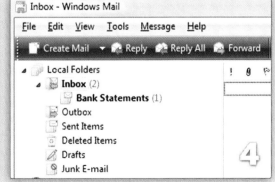

PLAN APPOINTMENTS AND MANAGE TASK LISTS WITH THE NEW WINDOWS
CALENDAR – IT HAS EVERYTHING YOU NEED TO KEEP ORGANISED.

Introducing Windows Calendar

While Apple users have had a decent calendar application built in for years, Vista's Calendar is the first one included with Windows. It's no token effort, either, covering both the basics of managing your own time and sharing that information with others. So it's well worth examining.

Like many other programs in Vista, Calendar is presented in a series of panes, each of which can be modified. The Navigation pane at the left shows a month planner, a list of your calendars (you can have up to 100) and a task list. In the centre is the calendar view itself, switchable between day, work week, seven-day week and month. You can overlay multiple calendars – perhaps separating work and home, or different family members – and compare them to avoid conflicts. The Details pane, at the far right, is where you fill in the specifics of each task or appointment. Along the top, there's a fairly sparse menu bar, with most common tasks shown in the toolbar below.

You can change how Calendar behaves by choosing Options from the File menu. It's worth personalising the default length of appointments and the hours of your work week, for starters, and you can tweak reminders to show up even when Calendar isn't running (this is off by default). If you travel regularly, you'll also want to enable support for time zones here – a feature you won't even find in most versions of Outlook.

SHARING This is all very helpful for keeping yourself organised from day to day, but the real power of Calendar becomes clear when you start sharing information with others. You can publish your calendar to a shared folder on your PC or network so that other users can see it (but not change it). If you've got some web space, you could upload it there for wider access, and Calendar will generate emails to send out to people you want to share it with.

Since Calendar supports the popular iCalendar standard (as used by Apple's iCal software), you can also invite attendees to your appointments via email, and these invitations will integrate with most other calendar programs on the market, including Microsoft Outlook. If you want, you can email your entire calendar in the same format: go to the Share menu and select Send by E-mail….

SUBSCRIBING The other benefit to being standards-compliant is that there are hundreds of calendars on the internet compiled by companies or individuals. You'll find everything from football fixtures and film releases to national holiday listings and celebrity birthdays. Some good places to start are www.icalshare.com and www.apple.com/macosx/features/ical/library. Once you're subscribed to these calendars, they'll stay synchronised to the online version, with new or updated events added automatically.

TIP

▶ You can assign each calendar its own colour, making it much easier to tell what's what when you've got several calendars overlaid in the Calendar view. Click on a calendar name and you'll see a drop-down menu appear in the Details pane. You can also sort your calendars into groups, which you can show and hide as necessary.

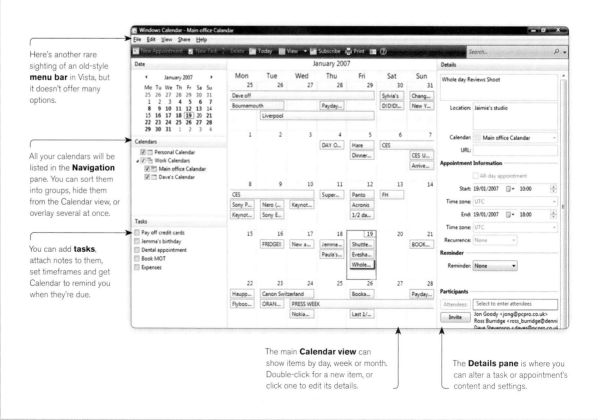

Here's another rare sighting of an old-style **menu bar** in Vista, but it doesn't offer many options.

All your calendars will be listed in the **Navigation** pane. You can sort them into groups, hide them from the Calendar view, or overlay several at once.

You can add **tasks**, attach notes to them, set timeframes and get Calendar to remind you when they're due.

The main **Calendar view** can show items by day, week or month. Double-click for a new item, or click one to edit its details.

The **Details pane** is where you can alter a task or appointment's content and settings.

HOW TO...
ARRANGE MEETINGS IN CALENDAR

If you're used to Outlook or a similar time-management app, Calendar shouldn't hold too many mysteries. Before emailing invites, though, it's worth checking that potential attendees have got iCalendar-compatible software to handle them.

1 **MAKE A DATE** Choose a day, week or month view using the View button in the toolbar. Then find the date you need, either using the month planner at the top left or by clicking Today in the toolbar: this will take you to the current date (indicated on the calendar by a red square, and on the month planner by a blue square), and you can navigate from there. Double-click on a time – or a date, in week or month view – and a new item will be created.

2 **SET DETAILS** Next, type a name for the appointment and move over to the Detail pane. You can add more specific information such as the location, as well as using the drop-down menu to alter which calendar you'd like the appointment to reside in. By default, everything is an 'All-day appointment', so untick this box if you need to enter a specific time to start or finish. If you've enabled the time zone feature in Options, you can set that here too. You can make the appointment recur daily, weekly, monthly or annually, or at more complex frequencies. If you want to set a reminder (which can go off minutes, days or weeks before the event), you should also tick the relevant setting in the File, Options menu to dictate whether you're alerted even if Calender isn't running at the time.

3 **ADD ATTENDEES** Go down to the Participants section. If the details of the people you want to invite are already in your Windows Contacts folder, you can just type each name in the Attendees box and their contact will appear in the list below. Otherwise, click on the box itself and you'll be able to add the relevant people and their details to your Windows Contacts list directly from there. Thanks to Vista's tight integration, these contacts will now be available in other apps, too.

4 **SEND INVITES** Click on Invite, and Calendar will make an appointment file for you and attach it to an email, which it will send to your intended participants using your default email program (such as Windows Mail). The message will contain all the necessary information about the event, including timing, location and any notes you've added. When attendees receive the email, the attached file, in .ics format, should open in their own calendar software, whether it's Windows Calendar or another iCalendar-compatible application. They'll then be able to suggest any changes and either accept or refuse the invitation. In turn, a response will be emailed back to you by their software and will update the details in Calendar.

HOW LONG?
Once you grasp the basics, you can set up meetings in seconds.

HOW HARD?
Microsoft has focused on making Calendar easy to use.

TIP

If you're not going to have access to your calendar for a few days, you can also print it out from the File menu. There aren't very many options, but you can specify a day, week or month view, and the results are presented in an impressively professional style.

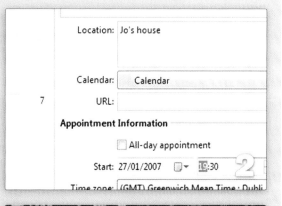

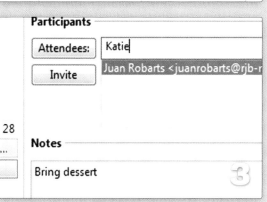

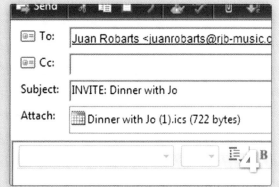

WINDOWS XP HANDLED IMAGE FILES WELL, BUT VISTA GOES FURTHER WITH
PHOTO GALLERY: A ONE-STOP SHOP FOR ORGANISING AND VIEWING PICTURES.

Introducing Photo Gallery

TIP

▶ If you've formed an unnatural attachment to the classic Windows Paint application – which has been around since the days of Windows 3.1 in the 1990s – don't worry, it's still there. It's in the same place it's always been, under Programs, Accessories, Paint. Or just type 'Paint' in the Instant Search box and it'll magically appear.

You'll initially find Windows Photo Gallery in the list whenever you hit the Start button. When you first open it, you'll be presented with a thumbnail preview screen, and by default you get a view of all the images in your Pictures folder. At the bottom of the window is a familiar-looking control bar, modelled on Windows Media Player, which lets you start a slide show, change the size of thumbnails, skip between images and so on. The interface looks great, and aside from one or two foibles it's a pleasure to use.

EASILY ORGANISED Naturally, Vista's all-pervading metadata tags (see p44) are integrated into Photo Gallery, making it simplicity itself to view only the shots taken in a particular month or with a custom tag you've defined, such as Kids or Holiday. All you need to do to filter the current view is click on a date, tag or star rating. You can filter by more than one category or tag, too: if you want to see just the holiday snaps you took in July, click on your Holiday tag, then hold Ctrl and click on July.

Photo Gallery integrates with the new Windows DVD Maker application (see p84) as well. Just select the pictures you want, hit the Burn button on the top menu bar and select Video DVD. This will launch Windows DVD Maker and allow you to create a disc that will play a slide show in any DVD-Video player.

SLIDE SHOWS AND THEMES At last, Windows has a decent built-in way to show off your photos. Hit the big button in the middle of the control bar at the bottom of the screen and the show begins. The slide show uses all the images in the current view, so you may first need to filter the view – for instance, by expanding the Tags filter on the left and clicking on a subject of your choice.

Alternatively, if you just want to show a few shots from the current view, you can select a group in the usual way: click on the first item, then hold Shift and click on the last, or Ctrl-click to select any number of individual images. Once your slide show has started, you can select a theme. The default option simply displays photos one after the other, but click on the Themes pop-up list at the bottom left of the slide show and you can make things a bit jazzier. Our favourite is Collage, which arranges several shots together at jaunty angles in scrapbook style.

Keen amateur photographers may get frustrated with Photo Gallery's image-manipulation tools, since they're largely automatic, with no advanced mode. But for anyone who likes to take snaps of family and friends, wants to keep track of them and occasionally likes to show them off, Photo Gallery is probably the only app you'll need.

Opposite, we introduce Photo Gallery's editing tools, while on p82 you can see how to import photos.

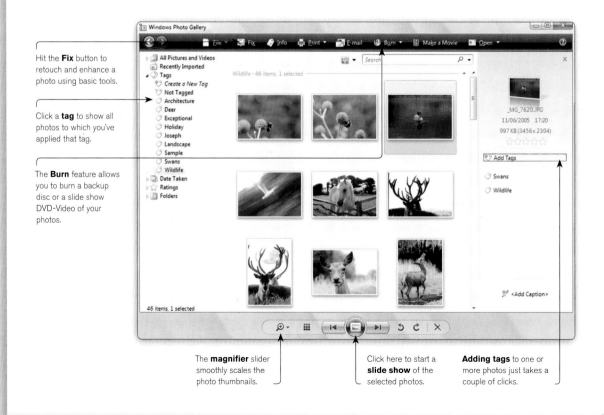

Hit the **Fix** button to retouch and enhance a photo using basic tools.

Click a **tag** to show all photos to which you've applied that tag.

The **Burn** feature allows you to burn a backup disc or a slide show DVD-Video of your photos.

The **magnifier** slider smoothly scales the photo thumbnails.

Click here to start a **slide show** of the selected photos.

Adding tags to one or more photos just takes a couple of clicks.

HOW TO...
ADD IMPACT TO YOUR PHOTOS

An estimated two billion digital photos were taken last year, so it makes sense for Windows to help out with your images. Fortunately, Windows Photo Gallery is up to the job. Here's a taste of what it can do for your snaps.

Photo Gallery offers a small but well-chosen selection of tools to help with the basics of photo retouching and enhancement. There are four categories of adjustments available: exposure, colour, cropping, and the red-eye fixer for removing those evil-looking pupils that people get when they look directly into the flash. There's also an Auto Adjust option that manipulates the other four controls as it sees fit to enhance your picture without human intervention. The operations are pretty self-explanatory, but we'll go through the process here so you can get a feel for what's possible. In particular, you should avoid Auto Adjust unless you're seriously pushed for time – it often gets things wrong.

1 **CHOOSE A PHOTO** To start, just click the image you want to adjust and then click on the Fix icon in the menu bar at the top of the Gallery view. This will open up your image with the Fix options displayed down the right-hand side of the screen.

2 **ADJUST EXPOSURE** A simple way to give a photo a bit more punch is to increase the contrast. As with most photo-editing and retouching operations, the secret is to go gently: a subtle change is almost always best. Click on Adjust Exposure,

which will show Brightness and Contrast sliders. Now click on the Contrast slider and drag it to the right a few notches. This won't work so well on indoor flash shots, since they tend to have pretty high contrast to start with, but outdoor photos that look a bit flat will often benefit.

3 **REMOVE RED-EYE** The red-eye reduction tool can be a lifesaver for those spur-of-the-moment party shots ruined by the Satan look. Again, to start the operation just click on the Red Eye option in the right-hand pane. Click and drag a rectangle around one of the eyes – preferably not both, although that does work most of the time. Do the same for the second eye if it needs it. Most of the time the red-eye fixer is pretty effective without any more intervention than this.

4 **REFINE THE RESULTS** If your initial red-eye correction doesn't work too well, bear in mind that it pays to be as accurate as possible when placing the rectangle. Click the Undo button at the bottom right and, before trying again, zoom in by clicking the magnifier icon at the bottom left of the control bar. Pan across to the eye by holding down the Alt key while dragging the image, then redraw the rectangle carefully around the pupil, avoiding the outer parts of the eye.

HOW LONG?
Fixing a photo can take seconds or hours; better results take longer.

HOW HARD?
The options are easy to apply, but successful adjustment takes skill.

TIP

Photo Gallery is integrated with the new Pictures screensaver. Right-click on a clear area of the Desktop, select Personalize and then Screensaver. Choose the Photos screensaver from the drop-down list and you can then select which photos to display by clicking Settings. You can select photos by tag, star rating or folder, and you can apply any of the Photo Gallery themes to your screensaver slide show.

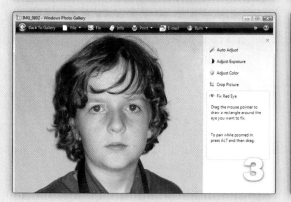

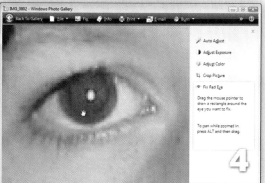

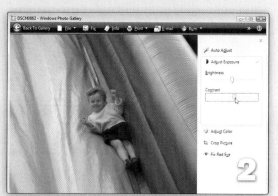

HOW LONG?
The whole process
should only take a
couple of minutes.

HOW HARD?
The downloading is
easy; tagging takes a
bit more effort.

HOW TO...
IMPORT AND TAG PHOTOGRAPHS

You won't get the best out of a digital camera if you leave your photos languishing on its memory card. Vista streamlines the process of transferring your pictures to the PC, and there's usually no need for any extra software to complicate matters.

In Windows XP, getting photos reliably from your camera often meant installing dedicated software supplied by its maker. But Vista's improved handling of USB devices extends to cameras, and with most modern models all you'll need to do is plug the camera into a USB port, switch it on and follow the steps described here. Vista does all the work, and your shots will be safely on your hard disk in minutes. Not only is there usually no need to install the third-party software that came with your camera, in fact it's preferable if you don't: leaving it to Vista is more reliable, and the more software you install, the more chance there is of your system getting clogged up and conflicts occurring. One exception is if you have a serious camera that uses RAW mode, which will require special software to process the images.

1 PLUG IN With a standard digital compact camera, when the camera is switched on and connected to the PC for the first time you'll see the familiar pop-up bubble notification from the System Tray, telling you it's locating drivers. Unlike with XP, you'll rarely be asked to insert a driver disc – again, Vista will cope with many different types of device all by itself. On future occasions the message won't appear. After a short while the Autoplay menu will pop up. This is essentially the same as in XP. To use Vista's import features, click the first option, 'Import pictures using Windows'.

2 IMPORT PHOTOS Vista will now search through the files on your camera. It'll ignore any it finds that have already been downloaded to your PC. If all the files have already been transferred, you'll get a message and the import process will end.

3 TAG AND BAG If there are new images (or videos), Vista will download them. But first, in true Vista style, it'll ask you for a tag to apply to the whole set. This can be invaluable later on, so get into the habit of giving your photo sessions meaningful tags.

4 VIEW THE RESULTS The download begins. If you've applied a tag, each image will be given that tag and placed in the Pictures folder in a new subfolder named with the tag plus today's date. If you didn't use a tag, the folder name is just the date, for example '10-02-2007'. You can tick 'Erase after importing' to clear the downloaded shots from your camera. Once the process completes, Photo Gallery will open.

WINDOWS DVD MAKER LETS YOU COMBINE VIDEOS AND PHOTOS TO WATCH ON
TV, COMPLETE WITH PROFESSIONAL-LOOKING MENUS AND SCENE SELECTION.

Introducing DVD Maker

Whether you've spent weeks carefully crafting a movie of your best friend's wedding, or simply want to distribute a selection of holiday photos to family and friends, Vista's DVD Maker will make your life easy. While the resulting disc may not quite look like the latest Hollywood blockbuster with whizzy 3D menu animations, you can put together a perfectly respectable DVD without spending hours mastering complex software.

DVD Maker won't start up unless your PC or notebook has a DVD writer, so you won't be able to create DVD projects on a computer without a drive and transfer it to another for burning. Usually, you'll enter DVD Maker after editing a video in Windows Movie Maker and choosing Publish to DVD.

SCREEN TEST The application essentially comprises two main screens. The first is where you select what you want to include on the disc, while the second is all about customising your creation and previewing it before you click the Burn button and make the real DVD.

The Add Files window at first appears a pretty desolate affair, but information and options are dotted around the edges. While options in DVD Maker are generally very limited, you can choose standard or widescreen formats (to match the type of TV you'll be

playing the movie on) and whether to display the menu, or simply play the movie when you put the DVD in.

On the next screen, called 'Ready to burn disc', you can choose the theme for your DVD. There are 20 of these 'Menu Styles' to choose from; many of them play video clips, or animation effects for photos, and are good enough to impress. You can also customise how buttons look (there's one for each scene in your movie) and change the menu text. While you can change the font and colour, though, you can't change its size. DVD Maker also lets you choose which videos play behind each menu, and music to go with it.

SLIDE SHOW Where photos have been added to your compilation, you can tweak slide show settings, including adding music and deciding which transition effect to use between each picture and how long to display each one. If you need to return to the previous screen, there's a large Back button, but it's easy to miss in the top corner.

You can choose to use a writable or rewritable DVD when you burn your movie. With a rewritable disc, you can erase and burn the movie again if it goes wrong. Not all DVD players are compatible with rewritable DVDs, however, so your DVD may not work with a particular player. Writable discs will almost always work.

TIP

▶ One of DVD Maker's less obvious options is DVD burning speed, which you can set to Fastest, Medium or Slow. The default is Fastest, but the Slow burn speed gives a better-quality result, so use this for an important movie such as a wedding. If you're using lower-quality DVDs – typically unbranded ones rather than premium brands such as Verbatim – they may skip if you use the Fastest setting, or last only a short time before they aren't recognised by the DVD player.

Customize menu allows you to tailor your chosen Menu Style to your liking, add your own text and so on.

The **Slide show** option lets you choose background music, adjust timing and set transition effects.

There are 20 **Menu Styles** to choose from, allowing you to match your presentation to the content of your movie.

Click **Preview** to go to the Preview screen, where you can test that your DVD menus are working correctly.

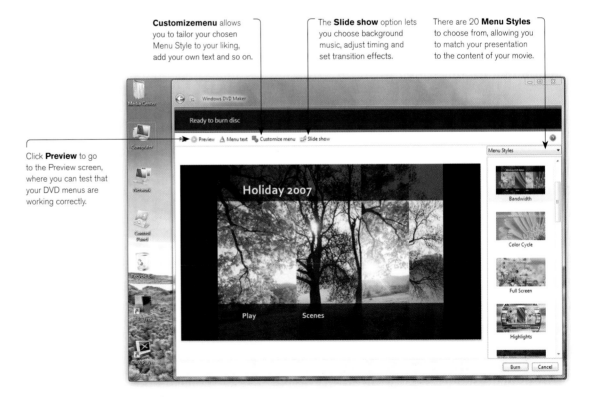

HOW TO...
MAKE A DVD WITH VISTA

DVD Maker steps you through the process of creating your DVD and does a lot of the hard work for you. All you have to do is customise the things you want to change and test that everything works before burning your disc.

1 ADD FILES Once you've clicked Next in DVD Maker's welcome screen, you'll be asked to add pictures and video to your DVD. If you've edited a video using Movie Maker (see p86), browse to your Videos folder and add the movie. This will create just one entry in DVD Maker's list, showing its duration on the right. You can add other videos and pictures to the list and reorder them by dragging. At the bottom you can enter a title, while a tiny pie chart on the left shows how many minutes (out of 150) you've used up. Click 'Options…' to access more settings, and make sure PAL is selected, not NTSC, if you want the DVD to work in UK/European (as opposed to US) DVD players.

2 CUSTOMISE MENUS Click Next and you can choose a Menu Style. Preview how each one will look with your movie by selecting it from the list. Click the 'Customize menu' button at the top to change the text shown in the menu, as well as the font and colour. You can change the Scenes button style, but the default Glass Rectangle is the best-looking option. At this point, you can also add foreground and background videos as well as choosing some music to play in the menus. The videos don't have to be part of your movie – you can select any videos on your hard disk.

3 SLIDE SHOW If you added digital photos in step 1, you should now click the Slide show button at the top of the screen. This takes you to a menu where you can change the transition between photos and opt to use pan and zoom effects (known in the trade as 'Ken Burns'). A word of warning, though: this isn't an intelligent setting, and often leaves large black borders visible as it zooms out of photos. Click the Preview button at the top of the screen to view your slide show and find out how your options look. The main box in this menu is where you add music to accompany your slide show. You can add as many songs as you like, and either manually select how long to display each picture or tick the box to automatically change the slide show length to match the length of the music.

4 PREVIEW The last step is to click the Preview button from the 'Ready to burn' disc screen. This lets you see the DVD as it will appear on TV. Click every menu button and scene selection to check all is functioning correctly. Use the virtual remote control buttons beneath the preview window to navigate, play, pause and skip chapters. Once you're happy, click OK at the bottom. Finally, insert a blank DVD into your DVD writer and click the Burn button to create the disc.

HOW LONG?
Once you get the hang of it, you'll be creating DVDs in minutes.

HOW HARD?
Straightforward, but check all your settings before burning.

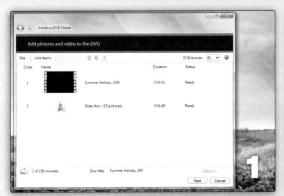

WITH THE COMBINATION OF WINDOWS MEDIA CENTER AND A TV TUNER,
YOU'LL NEVER NEED TO GET UP FROM YOUR SOFA AGAIN.

Introducing TV on your PC

TIP

▶ Recording TV is very hungry for disk space. It's not a big problem with today's large hard disk capacities, but an hour of TV takes up to 2GB, so older PCs may soon feel the strain. Media Center will warn you in advance if there isn't enough spare storage, but you can switch the recording location to an external or network disk if you like, and limit the space available for it to ensure there's enough for everything else you need on your PC. You can also set recordings to auto-expire (oldest first) when the space is needed or as soon as they're watched.

Even if you're convinced there's nothing worth watching on TV these days, chances are there's something on in the wee hours of the morning that will occasionally pique your interest. Equally, if don't have the time to sit and stare at whatever happens to be on, the features at the heart of Media Center could be just what you're looking for.

With a combination of sophisticated search facilities, support for multiple tuners and the flexibility to take recordings away with you on a portable device, you can skim off just what you want to watch, regardless of what time or channel it's on. It's TV for the 21st century. Adding a second tuner allows you to do even more: record two programmes at once (while still being able to watch a third, recorded programme), or watch a different channel while another records.

THE GUIDE Whether you're watching live or recorded TV, you can pause or rewind it, browse what's on now and next, or bring up a full-screen grid view – all with the picture carrying on behind it. You can also filter what's on offer using categories to see at a glance what's on over the next fortnight. Every day, Media Center will download 15 days of advance listings for each channel you can receive.

There's no need to mess around with timers or codes: use the Guide to browse, or use the search facilities

(see below) to find something you might be interested in later. Once you've found it, just press Record and Media Center will kick into action when the time comes. If what you want is a series, press the button again and it will record every episode with no further intervention. You can even set it to catch re-runs where possible. If your power options are set correctly, Media Center will automatically wake up your PC, record the programme and then shut it down again. The next time you come to it, the recordings will be sitting on your hard disk waiting for you. You can also skip through adverts, drag off a programme to a laptop or portable hard disk, burn it onto a DVD for backup (see p97), or watch it from another PC on your network.

DISCOVER A CHANNEL Using the Search option in the main menu (or from Recorded TV), you can scour the TV listings by title, keyword or category. Programme descriptions are catalogued, so if there's a subject you're interested in try the keyword search, or use it to find programmes featuring specific actors or directors. Category search is great for discovering programmes that might otherwise pass you by: you can browse by broad categories like sport, documentaries or children's, or follow these through to cricket, gardening or sitcom. There's a film section too, showing all the movies on for the next fortnight.

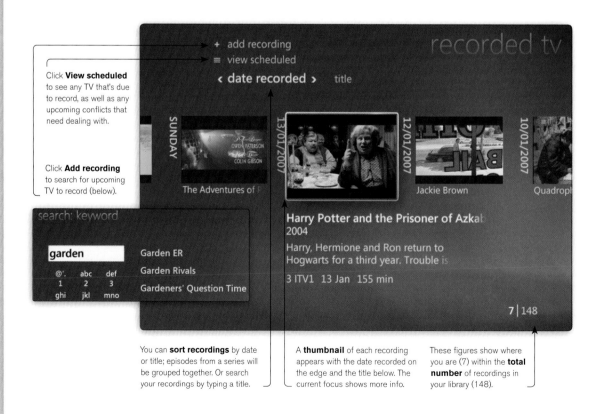

Click **View scheduled** to see any TV that's due to record, as well as any upcoming conflicts that need dealing with.

Click **Add recording** to search for upcoming TV to record (below).

You can **sort recordings** by date or title; episodes from a series will be grouped together. Or search your recordings by typing a title.

A **thumbnail** of each recording appears with the date recorded on the edge and the title below. The current focus shows more info.

These figures show where you are (7) within the **total number** of recordings in your library (148).

HOW TO...
ADD A TV TUNER

Many new PCs (and even notebooks) are now coming with TV tuners built in, but it's not difficult to add one to an existing system. If you've got a single tuner already, you can also use this method to install a second one.

1 **SELECT A TV TUNER** In the UK, we've got the simple choice between analogue or digital (DVB-T) tuners. The former can be used to receive the traditional five terrestrial channels, but these won't be around for much longer, so it makes more sense to opt for a hybrid or purely digital tuner – these give you the 70-odd channels of Freeview TV and radio available through your aerial (check www.freeview.com for coverage in your area). You can opt for an internal card or a USB version; the latter is much easier to install, but potentially untidy, and may not be quite as sensitive in low-signal areas. Whatever type you choose, make sure its drivers are compatible with Vista's Media Center before you buy, and install it after upgrading your PC to Vista if you're doing so. If you're adding a second tuner, a USB version is the safer bet to avoid any conflicts.

2 **LOAD THE DRIVERS** Before you've installed your internal PCI card or plugged in your USB tuner, make sure you have the right drivers downloaded from the manufacturer's website (or use the supplied CD). Then try running the installation software, taking note of what it tells you: if it says it can't find the device, turn your PC off and install it now, or it may happily install before asking you to power down and plug

in the tuner. Switch the PC back on and it should find and install everything it needs. Start up Media Center and go to the Set up TV option on the TV level of the menu, or go to Settings, TV, Set up TV signal.

3 **SET UP TV CHANNELS** Media Center will hold your hand for a while here: each step is preceded by an introduction screen, which you should read and click through. It will also go off and check details online at certain points. You'll need to confirm your region (it should be set to UK), confirm the tuners you want to use, then agree to the Guide terms and conditions – use a mouse here to prevent too much scrolling down. Finally, you'll enter your postcode and set your nearest signal provider, which you'll need to check yourself. Eventually, you'll get to scanning for the services you can receive. If you haven't already connected your rooftop or indoor aerial, now would be the time.

4 **SEE WHAT YOU'VE GOT** How many services you get will depend on the quality and positioning of your aerial, as well as the signal strength in your area. Once you're finished, you'll see the Live TV and Guide options appear in the Media Center menu. Check the Guide for the full line-up.

HOW LONG?
Less than an hour, including time to scan for TV stations.

HOW HARD?
Easy with an external tuner; an internal tuner will take more effort.

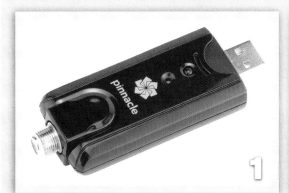

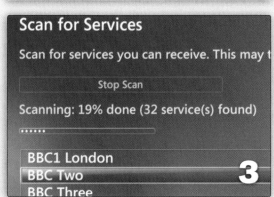

CONNECT YOUR XBOX 360 TO YOUR WINDOWS VISTA PC AND IT CAN ACCESS THE FULL MEDIA CENTER EXPERIENCE, INCLUDING RECORDED AND LIVE TV.

Using an Xbox 360 with Vista

When Microsoft first entered the gaming console wars with its Xbox series, we were far from certain how successful it would be. But its current incarnation, the Xbox 360, has proved to be one of the most popular products of its kind, and Microsoft has added further to its features over the last year. With high-definition music video and film trailers now available to download, plus the recent announcement of internet TV features, it's becoming a fully rounded home entertainment device in its own right.

But the real bonus for any Xbox owner with a PC running Windows Vista Home Premium or Ultimate is that you can use your Xbox as a Media Center Extender, accessing all the features of Media Center on your PC from your Xbox.

SETTING UP You'll need to have an Xbox Live account in order to connect to your PC. On the Xbox dashboard, go to Network Settings, Test Live Connection to check everything's running smoothly, and make sure you have the latest Xbox software update too. It's worth setting up the Media Center libraries as you want them on your PC, as this will save you repeating the job on your Xbox. Also make sure your PC's Network Category is set to Private to ensure your firewall is configured correctly.

Once that's done, you can go to the Xbox's Media menu and select the Media Center option. From there, the PC should find the Xbox and you'll be treated to a simple setup wizard. You'll be directed to download some software on your PC and add an eight-digit security code, but it's otherwise just a case of clicking through a couple of screens and letting Windows get on with it.

With the connection made, you can access the Media Center interface from your Xbox. You can even buy a remote control for it, but the Xbox controller works perfectly well too. Unlike previous generations of Media Center Extender, it behaves just as it would on the host computer, including smoothly scrolling menus, animations and even identical system sounds.

SHARE AND SHARE ALIKE Microsoft is making a concerted push to get the PC onto the radar of serious gamers. To that end, the Xbox Live service will soon be accessible through Windows Vista, allowing you to use one account for cross-platform games, and Windows and Xbox users to interact in-game by video, text or voice messaging. Even the Xbox 360's peripherals are Vista-compatible: the wired controller and steering wheel will simply plug into your PC's USB port, and there's a dongle to enable you to use the same wireless controller too.

FAQ

Q Is the Xbox 360 the only Media Center Extender product?

A Currently, yes, but look out for more in the near future. The technology is expected to find its way not only into dedicated set-top devices but to DVD players and even TVs. Vista supports up to five such devices. They should come in both wired and wireless variants, and can share the resources of the host PC: if you've got two TV tuners, for example, one can be used by the PC and one by the Extender.

Browse your Media Center library on your Xbox 360 as if you were at your PC. You'll get your pictures, music and video as usual – you can even schedule and watch TV programmes.

Introducing Ultimate Extras

DreamScene is the most initially impressive Ultimate Extra available so far. This 21st Century version of the Desktop wallpaper may not look very different in this picture, but rather than a static photo or pattern, DreamScene lets you run animated and video-based backdrops – in this case, drifting clouds. It comes with a selection of professionally made, seamlessly looping video backgrounds, but you can also use any video file you like. You might find your wobbly family home videos make you feel a bit queasy if they're constantly looping on the Desktop, though.

TIP

▶ Only owners of Vista Ultimate Edition will get access to the exclusive Windows Ultimate Extras. These aren't installed with the operating system; they're made available for download afterwards as part of the Windows Update routine in Ultimate. The range of Ultimate Extras should increase over time, with five available at launch.

GroupShot is a great-looking application that uses the best parts of similar pictures to make a new photo. It's mainly focused on getting a decent picture of everyone in a group, hence the name. Imagine you've taken three or four shots of your whole family in one sitting: in one of them your mum has her eyes closed; in another someone's looking at their feet. GroupShot allows you to identify which areas you like, and combines them so that everyone gets a flattering portrait.

Proof that poker has entered the mainstream couldn't get much more positive than Windows gaining a poker game. **Hold 'Em** recreates the most popular version of the game of chance, and starts you out with one thousand (unfortunately fake) dollars. The surprising part is that you can't play against others online: Hold 'Em can only be played against up to five computer opponents, which severely dents its appeal. Nonetheless, if you want to practice your tactics before (or instead of) venturing into the merciless world of real gambling, it's worth a look.

Ultimate and Enterprise ship with BitLocker hard disk encryption, and the BitLocker Drive Preparation tool will create the necessary disk partition without requiring third-party software. Just in case you lose your encryption keys, Secure Online Key Backup lets you store them safely. Remember, without the key, encrypted data is lost forever.

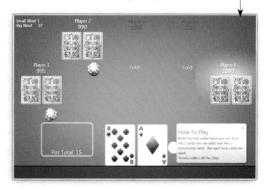

HOW TO...
SYNC DEVICES WITH MEDIA CENTER

You can use Media Center to synchronise music to your MP3 player. It doesn't support iPods (you'll have to use Apple's own iTunes for that), but just about every other digital music device will work, along with some mobile phones and PDAs.

HOW LONG?
Depends on how many tracks you need to organise and transfer.

HOW HARD?
Pretty simple, bar a few possible wrinkles the first time you plug in.

TIP

▶ If you want more control over your music selection, you can also use Windows Media Player to do the same job. Go to the Sync tab and, using your mouse, drag and drop files to the Sync Pane on the right. Unlike with Media Center, you won't be prompted to save it as a playlist, so if you want to use that collection of tracks in the future make sure you use the Save as Playlist option in the Sync List before syncing to your device.

1 **ADD TO QUEUE** The first step is to create a playlist of the tracks you want to transfer, so go to the music library in Media Center. Use the various browse views to find the artists, albums or tracks you'd like to add, or search directly by typing the name. You can click through to individual albums or songs and use the Add to Queue button, or use a mouse to right-click and select Add to Queue. If you're using a remote, the 'i' button performs the same function as a right-click in Media Center.

2 **SAVE AS PLAYLIST** Once you've got everything you're looking for, go back to the main menu and select Now Playing and Queue. From there, select View Queue, which will display a list of everything you've just added. Choose the Save as playlist button on the left-hand side, and you'll be prompted to give it a name – you may find dating it will prove handy too. You'll also be able to call up this playlist in the future from either Media Center or Windows Media Player.

3 **SYNC TO DEVICE** Now that's done, you can plug in your device. If it's the first time you've connected it, wait for the drivers to install

– this should happen automatically (if not, you may have to come out of Media Center to do it). You should then be asked whether you want to sync media content to the device. Click Yes. If this doesn't happen automatically, you can also go to Settings | Sync. You'll then be taken to step 4. If you've synchronised with this device before, it will automatically start synchronising using the settings you used last time, adding any new playlists you've made to the top. If you want to change these settings, click Edit List before it starts transferring content across.

4 **MANAGE YOUR LIST** The Manage List screen displays all of your playlists ordered by date, so the one you've just created should be at the top. You can edit this list if you like, using the 'X's to remove items you don't want and the up/down arrows to change the relative priorities; it's very intuitive in practice. In its default state, Media Center will go down the list until the device is full. If the same song is on multiple playlists, it should only be copied across once. You can also use the Add More button to browse your library for more content to synchronise. If your device supports it, you can add photos or videos too.

HOW TO...
BURN A DVD WITH MEDIA CENTER

Once you've got all those files on your PC, they aren't stuck there: one of the easiest ways of moving them about or backing them up is to burn them to CD or DVD, and you can do that directly from Media Center's interface.

CHOOSE YOUR FORMAT There are several ways of creating a compilation DVD in Windows Media Center, but the simplest is to go to the main menu and select Burn CD/DVD from the Tasks section. If you've got a blank DVD in your optical drive, you'll get three different options: Data DVD, Video DVD or DVD Slide Show. If it's a blank CD, you'll just be offered Audio CD or Data CD (see Tip, right) if you're not sure which to opt for. In this case, we're going to put some of our recorded TV onto a Video DVD, but the basic process is much the same regardless of which disc type you choose.

NAME YOUR COMPILATION You have to name your compilation right at the start (although you can come back and change it at the end). You can then specify where you want to get your files from; for our Video DVD, we're given the choice between the Video library or Recorded TV sections, and we'll opt for the latter. For a data CD or DVD, you'll be able to archive TV, music or video, whereas an audio CD will only give you the option of choosing from your music library.

ADD THE FILES The Library screen you're taken to is slightly adapted from the normal one, with each item having a small checkbox next to it to indicate whether or not it's part of the compilation yet. As we're using a single-layer DVD, we can only fit one of these TV episodes on it, although Media Center does offer the option of scaling back the quality slightly to fit more onto the disc. In this case, we've decided that's fine, so we've been able to add the second episode. You'll still reach a stage where you can't fit any more on the disc, though, and Media Center will warn you of this with a dialog box. You can also keep an eye on how much space remains with the indicator at the bottom left of the screen.

NOW BURN You can now review your compilation, rename the individual items where appropriate, or move the items around: here, the two episodes we've chosen will play back-to-back on a DVD player as separate chapters. Before you commit to disc, you can also opt to go back and add or remove items, or start the whole process again. Once you OK this, the disc will start burning, and you can either wait for it or click OK and go back to doing something else in Media Center. The PC will need to convert these files to a different format before actually burning them to the disc, so this process may take an hour or two.

HOW LONG?
Not long to set up, but the burning process can drag on for a while.

HOW HARD?
You're led through the task, but make sure you choose the right format.

TIP

If you opt for a data disc, Media Center will burn files just as they're stored on your PC, so it's ideal for backup. But you'll only be able to read them on a PC. Audio CDs are in the standard CD format: 79 minutes of audio, regardless of any MP3 compression on your files. A Video DVD will be compatible with DVD players, fitting 120 minutes on a single-layer disc or 220 on double-layer. A DVD Slide Show puts digital photos and video onto a DVD with a soundtrack, much like Windows DVD Maker (see p84).

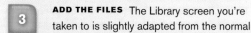
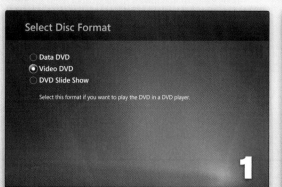

VISTA STILL HAS OLD FAVOURITES LIKE SOLITAIRE AND HEARTS, BUT IT'S UPPED
THE STAKES WITH SOME RATHER EXCELLENT NEW GAMES. HERE'S OUR PICK.

Vista's bundled games

There are ten levels to choose from in **Chess Titans**, from the easily beatable (anything up to Level 3) to the rather more tricky (we struggled above Level 7). The graphics are very easy on the eye and make reading the board surprisingly similar to real life. Unlike with commercial games, you don't get any coaching facilities, there's no way to rate your ability or keep a record of games, and there are no networking options. The only stats on offer are about how many games you've won and lost (plus winning and losing streaks), split per level. Even so, for a bundled game, it's surprisingly slick: a highlight is the way you can rotate the board in three dimensions.

You can find each game by typing its name into the Search bar, or type 'games explorer' and you'll see all the installed games. You'll also get an at-a-glance guide to any age restrictions associated with each game, and an indication – via the performance rating for your computer, and the performance rating for the game – as to how well it will actually play. You can also get to the games in the Media Center via the More Programs menu.

This one's definitely for the kids. Three mini games are represented by houses in **Purble Place**. In the house with purple frosting, you race against time to bake a cake by matching pictures of the required ingredients. There's also a pairs game, and finally a Mr Potato Head-type exercise where you add eyes, mouth and nose to get the right combination.

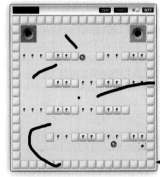

InkBall is a frankly bizarre game where you have to guide coloured balls into their respective holes using squirts of ink, controlled by a mouse or ideally a Tablet PC's stylus. Squirt as much ink as you like, and when a ball hits the line it disappears. The game's over when a ball goes into the wrong hole. It's simple but strangely compulsive, and appeals to younger kids too.

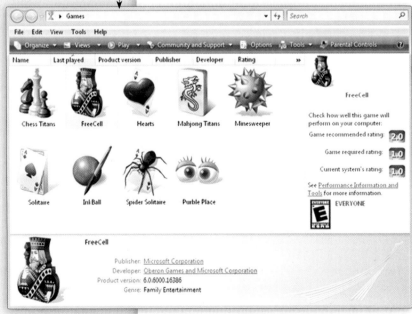

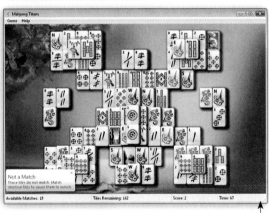

Mahjong Titans is another very slick offering that will no doubt appeal to all Mahjong addicts – and create a few new ones. Match a pair of tiles and they disappear, but you can't match blocked tiles (ones that can't be slid out without disturbing another). There are six games to choose from, and you can view stats on each type, including your win ratio and high scores. A nice touch is that you can change the look of the tiles: children will like the cartoony Pastel Tiles option.

The **Ultimate** Vista™ Experience
gaming • photos • video

Windows Vista™ Ready*

ATI Certified†

- Enjoy **stunning visuals** as your PC comes alive with over 1 billion colors
- Experience **high performance** and the ability to run more applications faster
- Rediscover your memories in **HD** when viewing your photos and videos
- Unleash the **ultimate gaming experience** with high speed action and lifelike characters

So what are you waiting for? Get ATI™ today and get the Ultimate Vista Experience!

connect3D

www.connect3d.com

ATI Radeon™ X1650

The ATI Connect3D Radeon™ X1650 series is designed to deliver outstanding digital entertainment and 3D graphics through its unique ultra-threaded architecture and Avivo™ video and display technology.

ATI Radeon™ X1300

From playing games and surfing the Internet to watching digital video and editing photographs, the ATI Connect3D Radeon™ X1300 series breathes life into the graphics of all your media applications.

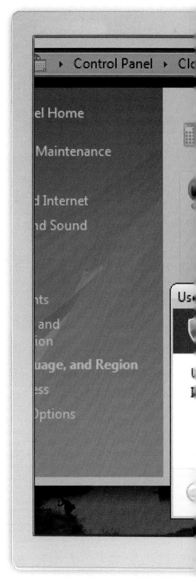

CHAPTER **8**

STAYING SAFE IN

There's nothing more important in the computing universe of today than security, and Vista attempts to cover almost all the bases. Spyware is held at bay by Windows Defender. Hackers are kept out of your system with a new and significantly stronger version of Windows Firewall. To provide a last line of defence, the brand-new User Account Control will ask your

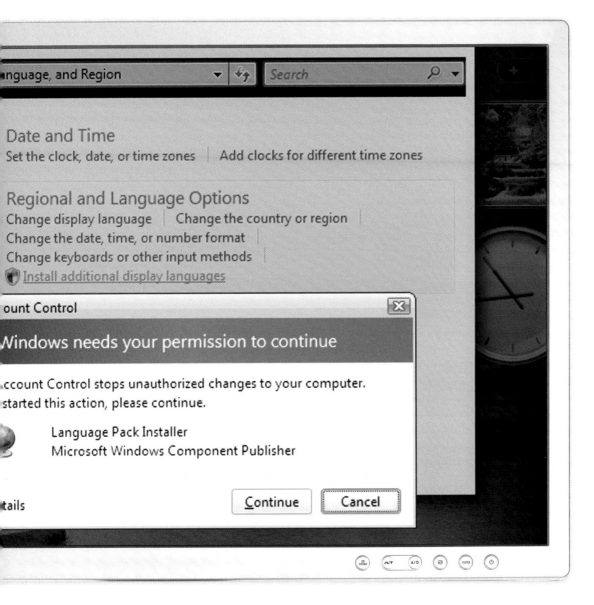

VISTA

permission before executing any program that could damage your system. And Windows finally gets a backup utility worthy of the name. Most important of all to anyone with a family are the new Parental Controls, which allow you to restrict your children's access to the internet – and perhaps in turn restrict access to those on the outside with bad intentions.

VISTA IS THE MOST SECURE VERSION OF WINDOWS EVER. WRITTEN FROM THE
GROUND UP TO KEEP HACKERS, THIEVES AND OTHER THREATS AT BAY.

Introducing Security Center

Microsoft has paid a lot of attention to security in Windows Vista. Not only has it improved and added to the security tools that came with Windows XP, it's actually built the whole operating system using a new, more secure architecture. Even if a virus or spyware file manages to get past Vista's defences, the amount of damage it can do is now vastly reduced.

This is partially thanks to User Account Control, which acts as a safeguard against malicious software secretly taking control of your system. You'll be warned when any such programs try to make changes to your system, and can deny them access. Although we broadly welcome User Account Control, it isn't perfect. The message it provides usually lacks any meaningful detail, so many people will still throw caution to the wind and click Continue, allowing the software to install. But even so, it's better than no warning at all. For more about User Account Control, see over the page.

Another big advantage is that Vista makes it far easier to use a Standard Account than Windows XP did with its equivalent Limited Account. When you log in as a Standard user, it will allow you to do all the day-to-day jobs, such as running most programs and deleting your own files, but not access anyone else's files, install or uninstall software or delete files that the computer needs to run. Games, which rarely ran with a Limited Account, should work too. Even experts should use a Standard Account when they don't perform admin-related tasks.

MALWARE PROTECTION Despite early rumours, there's no dedicated anti-virus software built into Vista. You'll either have to find a third-party application yourself or sign up to Microsoft's Windows Live OneCare service, once it's launched in the UK. However, Vista does include the Windows Defender utility, which claims to repel malicious software such as spyware and viruses. Although it's handy to have this preinstalled on a new computer, we'd recommend that most people augment it with a fully featured anti-virus program (see p108 for details on how to download and install one for free). And for more about setting up Windows Defender, see our complete guide on p116.

FIREWALL Windows Vista comes with a more powerful firewall than the one included with Windows XP. At first glance, it looks identical, but the main improvement is that it can now restrict outgoing connections as well as incoming traffic. The firewall is good enough to let you get up and running with your new system, but it won't necessarily withstand the most determined attacks.

The main benefit the Vista firewall will bring to most people is that you can now enable or disable the firewall on different network interfaces, such as wireless and physical network connections, from a single screen. This makes it less likely you'll forget to run unprotected, and quicker to disable the firewall should you eventually decide to install a more fully featured third-party firewall that

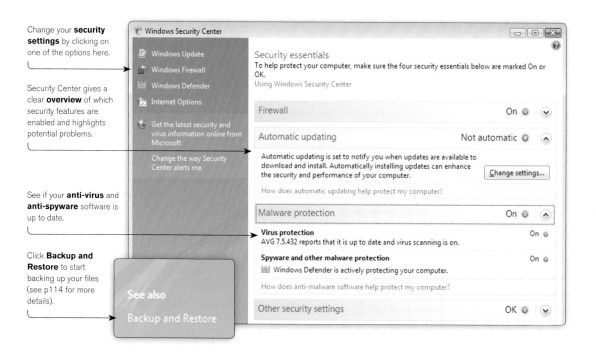

Change your **security settings** by clicking on one of the options here.

Security Center gives a clear **overview** of which security features are enabled and highlights potential problems.

See if your **anti-virus** and **anti-spyware** software is up to date.

Click **Backup and Restore** to start backing up your files (see p114 for more details).

See also
Backup and Restore

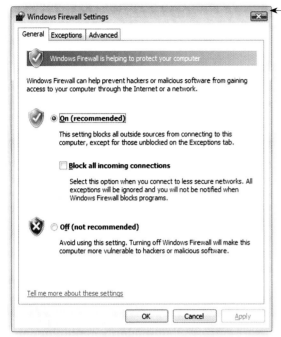

Vista's built-in **firewall** can prevent other computers making connections to yours. It creates an obstacle for attackers, including hackers and malicious programs such as internet worms. You can allow incoming connections to certain programs, which is necessary to play some online games or use Internet Messaging (IM) programs like Windows Live Messenger. If you need to use your PC on an untrusted network, you can quickly prevent all incoming connections by ticking Block all incoming connections.

Windows Update doesn't just let you download automatic security upgrades, it also provides access to updates for other Microsoft products and extra features that may be made available. It can display a full list of all updates that have been installed since your PC was first used, and if you find that an update is causing problems you can uninstall it. You can also choose to ignore and hide some updates, or unhide them if you later decide to use them.

Not only does **Windows Defender** attempt to intercept malicious software and prevent it running, it can also let you see details of all the software running on your system. The Software Explorer option can display all of the programs that are loaded when Windows first starts up, the currently running programs, software that's connected to the network, and system-level programs that give network access to regular applications. A Quarantine area stores suspicious files that have been caught and stopped from running, and there's an Allowed items list where you can specify programs that Defender should ignore.

supports application control. Application control lets you decide which programs can and can't access the internet, a task that any personal firewall program worth its salt can handle, but Windows' still can't.

AUTOMATIC UPDATING Keeping your applications and operating system up to date is critical if you want to avoid being an easy target for hackers and the malicious software they use to attack computer systems. Security holes are frequently being found and exploited in office programs like Word and Excel, and internet software like Internet Explorer, Outlook and Firefox, not to mention core parts of operating systems. Microsoft aims to fix these by issuing updates that you can download and install. To avoid you having to remember to do this regularly, Windows Vista (like XP) can do it automatically.

You can choose to have updates downloaded and installed quietly in the background, or opt to be notified when they've been downloaded and are ready to be installed. Alternatively, you can choose to be notified when there are updates available and decide for yourself if and when to download them, or you can take the least wise choice and disable updates completely. We'd only recommend this last setting if you want to work on the internet temporarily using a slow connection such as GPRS (via a mobile phone) or a good old-fashioned dial-up modem.

INTERNET SECURITY SETTINGS Internet Explorer has a whole raft of new settings, plus the ability to apply them to different zones such as the internet, on a local network and with trusted sites. There are new tools to prevent you falling foul of phishing attacks, where hackers pose as legitimate sites or services requesting your private details, and a new Protected Mode means that, even if a rogue virus manages to penetrate your defences, it will run at a low level of

privileges and therefore be less able to do damage. You can find more about Internet Explorer's security features in our step-by-step guide to connecting to the internet safely, starting on p66.

PARENTAL CONTROLS Parental Controls are a brand-new addition to Windows Vista, providing a powerful way to protect other users of your computer. Not only can you track how other members of your family are using the internet, you can also restrict what type of sites they can visit, the type of games they can play (according to age rating) and which applications they can use. You can even limit the time periods during which the PC will work.

The Web Filter can be as restrictive as you like, allowing only specified sites, or you can opt for a more basic level of protection. This doesn't just prevent certain sites from being visited: entering inappropriate search terms into search engines will also result in a blank page. You can completely block the ability to download files too.

ENCRYPTION Like Windows XP Professional, Vista supports the Encrypting File System (EFS). EFS lets you encrypt individual files and folders so that other users of your computer can't access documents that need to be kept private. Vista now provides the ability to store your encryption keys on a smart card, making it easier to use encryption. The downside is that EFS is only available in Vista Home Premium and higher versions.

Windows Vista also has a new hard disk encryption system, BitLocker, available in the Enterprise and Ultimate editions. This allows you to encrypt your entire hard disk, making it useless to thieves if they steal it from the computer. You can also secure it further so that you need to provide a PIN or insert a USB key to unlock the PC. This is particularly useful for laptops, which are more likely to be lost or stolen – a recovery key can be stored in various ways in case you lose the key.

VIA THE INTERNET, YOU MAY COME INTO CONTACT WITH VIRUSES, SPYWARE,
TROJANS AND OTHER THREATS. HERE'S HOW TO STOP THEM IN THEIR TRACKS.

Introducing virus protection

FAQ

**Q How do I know that
my computer isn't
already infected with
a virus or spyware?**

A It's in the nature of
computer viruses to
spread, so if your system
is infected the virus will
attempt to infect your
friends and colleagues.
In some cases, they may
receive an infected email
from you, but viruses
often change the email
address of the sender,
so you may have to look
out for other symptoms.
These typically include
a reduction of your
PC's performance and
maybe a slow internet
connection. The same
goes for spyware, which
is particularly likely to
reduce PC performance.

Viruses and other malicious software form one of the
biggest threats faced by your PC. Although Windows Vista
contains various built-in security mechanisms designed
to reduce the impact of a virus, it's better if you can avoid
such things completely, or at least have your computer
detect them before they can run. To do this, you need to
install anti-virus software.

Until quite recently, the most likely way you
would encounter a virus was to receive it as an email
attachment. While email viruses are still going strong, a
new threat has emerged. Spyware – software designed to
steal your personal information – is becoming increasingly
widespread, and it tricks its way onto your computer by
pretending to be something useful (ironically, often by
masquerading as an anti-spyware utility) or something
pornographic, or it may even attempt to install itself
invisibly as you visit an infected website. Most anti-virus
programs now claim to detect spyware as well as viruses.

On the opposite page, we show you how to
download and install a free anti-virus program for Windows
Vista. All of the big anti-virus brands provide Vista-
compatible anti-virus software too, but we've never seen a
product that's able to detect 100% of viruses, trojans and
other threats. To keep your PC safe from infection, you
also need to be aware of the dangers and act sensibly.

AVOIDING VIRUSES For a start, ensure that User Account
Control (UAC) is enabled – see p106. If malware attempts
to activate, UAC will ask if you want the program to run
and you can refuse it permission. But how do you stop a
virus getting onto your system in the first place?

To stop email viruses coming your way, your
internet service provider (ISP) may have an optional anti-
virus service to ensure infected attachments never arrive.
Even if they do, they can't activate until you click them, so
exercise caution when opening an attachment – even from
someone you know. The clue will be in the message that
comes with it. If it doesn't read like it's from your friend,
colleague or family member, it won't hurt to reply and ask
if they really sent it. Don't open it until they confirm.

Even the basic firewall software that comes with
Vista will repel internet worms, programs that try to attack
vulnerable PCs. If you have a broadband connection and
use a router, its built-in firewall should also handle these
threats, but it still makes sense to use a software firewall
too, particularly if you use public wireless networks.

Finally, avoid the darker areas of the internet.
Sites that offer adult content, stolen software licence codes
and ripped-off movies are likely offenders. If you want to
download security software, ensure you go directly to the
company's official website and not a fake.

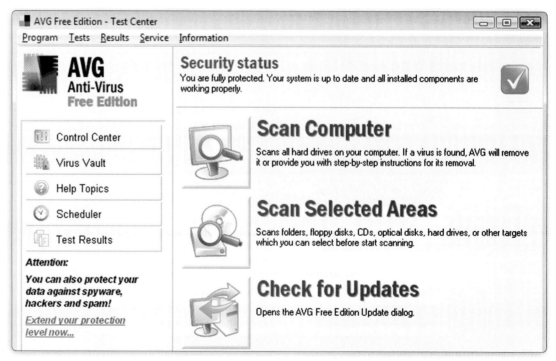

AVG Anti-Virus Free Edition is well equipped and frequently updated. It's a great way to add virus protection to Windows Vista for free.

HOW TO...
INSTALL AN ANTI-VIRUS PROGRAM

Home users can get reasonable protection for free. Although Windows doesn't provide a full anti-virus program, Grisoft has one that's freely available to download. Make this the first site you visit when you get your new Vista PC.

1 **DOWNLOAD AVG ANTI-VIRUS** Get the free version from http://free.grisoft.com. It's suitable for Windows Vista systems running on 32-bit platforms. Click on AVG Anti-Virus Free and scroll down the page that loads. You now have two options. If you intend to use the software on a business PC, or you use a 64-bit version of Vista, you'll need to click Download commercial version – AVG Anti-Virus Professional Edition costs £19 for a year. Otherwise, click Download free version. Yet another page will load, providing a link to the actual program. Click this to download it.

2 **RUN THE INSTALLER** Once the download completes, run the program to install AVG. When asked, choose Standard Installation. The installation procedure then helps you set up the software by offering choices to update with the latest virus databases, scan your disk and register with Grisoft. Before running the update, click the Internet button to get the latest files from Grisoft's website. If you tick the option above this, the program will always get updates from the internet when available. This is a wise choice, but you can always change it later. Let the updates install themselves, as this will increase the anti-virus software's accuracy.

3 **SET UP DAILY SCAN** At this point, you can decide whether or not to run a scheduled scan every day. This probably isn't necessary, because a good anti-virus program should detect viruses as soon as they arrive, rather than picking them up after they've infected your system. However, you can schedule the daily scan for a time when your PC isn't usually busy (but will be left switched on). So if you often leave your PC on and unsupervised for long periods, setting a scheduled scan won't hurt. You can also set the daily virus scan so it runs at a low priority. This means it will take longer to complete, but won't slow down any other applications you may be using at the time. Alternatively, untick the box to choose no daily scan.

4 **PERFORM YOUR FIRST SCAN** AVG will now ask if you want to scan your computer right away. If you have the time, click the Scan Computer button. Alternatively, if you don't want to tie up your computer at the moment with a task that could take quite a long time, click Next instead. When you want to run a scan, just click the massive Scan Computer button on AVG's main control panel. If it detects any viruses, let it store them safely in the Vault area, which imprisons the bad files and prevents them from harming your PC.

HOW LONG?
After the 20MB download, setup should only take minutes.

HOW HARD?
Easy, but remove any pre-installed anti-virus software first.

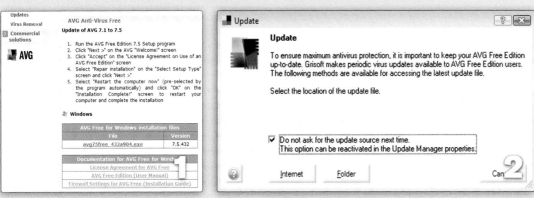

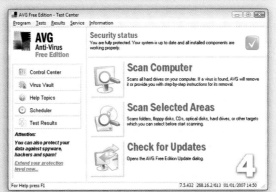

TO PROTECT YOUNGER MEMBERS OF YOUR FAMILY, NOTHING BEATS PERSONAL SUPERVISION. WHEN THIS ISN'T POSSIBLE, VISTA HAS THE NEXT BEST THING.

Introducing Parental Controls

Many security features are enabled by having different user accounts for each person who has access to your PC. Most of these are aimed at preventing mischievous or unfortunate people from messing up your settings or installing malware, but Parental Controls is designed to protect their own welfare. You can control how long someone spends using Windows, which programs they can run and what websites they can visit. You can also view reports to find out how your PC has been used.

TIME LIMITS For every user on whom you impose Parental Controls, you can set limits on how long they can spend using the computer. Setting the available hours is as simple as clicking on or dragging across cells in the weekly timetable grid. When their time is up, users won't just be dumped out of Windows – warnings will appear running up to the deadline. Should someone carry on working regardless, they'll be logged out, but their work will be saved. Once logged out, a user can't log back in until the next available time slot.

WEB FILTERS At its strictest, Parental Controls' Web Filter system will only allow users to visit a list of sites specified by you. You can even tick a box to prevent them from downloading files. If you think this is too harsh, you can use the automatic blocking system and add specific sites that you want to block to another list. Setting up automatic blocking is a simple matter of choosing the web restriction level. The options range from None through Medium to High. A custom option lets you pick subjects to block, such as pornography, drugs and weapons.

Even searching for dubious terms using popular search engines will cause the Web Filter to kick in. This prevents clever users from bypassing your pornography controls by visiting Google Images, for example. However, the filter isn't a panacea, and there are some strange contradictions in its results. For instance, searching for 'abortions' is permitted, but 'condoms' is blocked. 'Musket' is blocked, but it's easy to find information about the more modern 'M16' assault rifle.

PROGRAM CONTROLS The Applications Restrictions section lets you decide which programs a user can run. Some will be obvious choices, such as a word processor, a web browser and maybe an email client. You'll also need to enable third-party security software such as your anti-virus scanner. Blocking Internet Messaging clients like Windows Live Messenger is down to your judgement. You can also stop users from playing certain games, either specifically or using categories such as age rating and content type.

TIP

If you change Parental Control settings for a user currently logged in, these won't be enforced until they log out and in again. But you can force their session to close, even without their password. Open the Task Manager by pressing <Ctrl-Alt-Del> and click the Users tab. Select the username and click Logoff. If that fails, click the Processes tab and tick Show processes from all users. Select each one that belongs to the user and click End Process, then try logging them off again. They may lose unsaved work.

Click to **turn on or off** Parental Controls for this user. Your settings are remembered while turned off.

Activity reports show what users get up to.

Use the **Web Filter** to dictate which sites are accessible to this user and which are banned.

Click to set **time limits** on this user's access to the computer.

You can automatically **block unsuitable programs** while allowing essential ones to run.

Your **current settings** for this user are summarised here for quick reference.

HOW TO...
SET UP PARENTAL CONTROLS

Setting up Parental Controls is easy. You can simply apply a general policy for your users, or customise it as much as you want. All the options can be disabled individually too, making this a flexible way to control how your PC is used.

1 **WEB FILTERING** To enable the Web Filter, click the option 'Block some websites or content'. Unless you already have a long list of acceptable sites in mind, it's less work to use automatic blocking. Choose a security level, bearing in mind that High blocks every site except those rated suitable for children. If you want to prevent users from downloading files, tick the 'Block file downloads' box at the bottom of the page. If you have a short list of sites you know you don't want visited, click 'Edit the Allow and block list' and enter their details.

2 **SET TIME LIMITS** Build a timetable to dictate when the PC will be available to this user. Dragging the cursor across Allowed time slots makes them unavailable. Repeating the process reverts to Allowed. You have a week's schedule to play with, so it's easy to stop the PC being used late on school nights and extend the time during the weekend, for example. No-one will lose the data they're working on if they continue past the deadline, but they'll have to stop working.

3 **CONTROL GAMING** The Games control panel lets you decide what specific games are allowed, as well as choosing types based on their content and age restrictions. The easiest option is to use the age rating system. Click the maximum age rating you consider appropriate for each user. Bear in mind that not every game has a built-in rating. If you want to block all unrated games too, tick the option at the top of the screen called 'Block games with no rating'. For extra customisation, tick the content type options to block games that include, for example, references to drugs, sex or fear. Again, this relies on the game having official specifications available.

4 **CREATE EXCEPTIONS** If you need to make exceptions to your rules, open the option labelled 'Allow and block specific programs'. Scroll through the list of programs installed on your PC and tick the ones this user is allowed to run. Include essentials like anti-virus software and perhaps useful utilities such as Adobe Acrobat Reader. You can block games you know to be unsuitable by ensuring they're not ticked. If you have older, unrated games you don't want to ban, tick them. If you don't see the program you want, click Browse and try to find it. Alternatively, log into the user's account and run the program from there. If Windows has any doubt, it will ask for the administrator password. After entering it, you can choose to always block or always allow the program.

HOW LONG?
Ten minutes, although you could spend hours tinkering with settings.

HOW HARD?
Easy. Resisting pleas to slacken your controls might prove trickier.

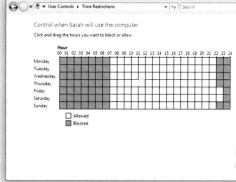

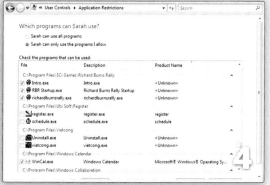

KEEPING UP TO DATE WITH WINDOWS' SECURITY PATCHES CAN BE A TEDIOUS
PROCESS. VISTA'S AUTOMATIC UPDATES FEATURE TAKES THE PRESSURE OFF.

Introducing Windows Update

Hackers seem to find new ways to break into Windows on a weekly basis. To counteract their attacks, Microsoft regularly releases updates to close these holes. You need to apply these updates immediately to minimise the chances of anyone gaining unauthorised access to your computer. Fortunately, Windows Vista can take care of this for you.

Microsoft also releases updates that just make Windows more stable. Like the security fixes, these are classified as 'important'. By default, Vista will download and install all available important updates, as well as 'recommended' updates, which might include new software drivers for peripherals and built-in hardware such as network interfaces and graphics cards. Previously, recommended updates had to be downloaded manually. Now you can keep your PC fully up to date automatically.

DO IT YOURSELF If you prefer to make your own decisions about what drivers are installed on your PC (and we certainly wouldn't blame you), you can disable the automatic installation of recommended updates. Open Control Panel, choose Windows Update, click 'Change settings', then untick the 'Recommended updates' option.

You can go a step further and stop even important updates from being downloaded and installed automatically. Here, you have two choices: the first is 'Download updates but let me choose whether to install them'. This is fine if you have a broadband internet connection and you want to tell the updates to install once you've finished using your PC for a while. Alternatively, you can let Windows notify you when updates are available, but prevent it from downloading or installing them. This is sensible if you're a mobile user who pays for wireless internet access, for example. The option you need is 'Check for updates but let me choose whether to download and install them'.

Whichever setting you choose, something may go wrong when Windows attempts to download and install an update. If that happens, you'll get a message warning you about the failure, and you can try again.

REMOVING AN UPDATE If you suspect that an update has started making your PC misbehave, you can remove it. Only do this if you're sure the update is to blame, or you could be opening a security hole. Click the 'View update history' link in Windows Update and, at the top of the window that appears, click 'Installed updates'. Right-click the update you want to remove and click the Uninstall option when it pops up. You can also find this list by opening Control Panel, clicking on Programs and Features, then choosing 'View installed updates'.

View your **history** to check out which updates you've already installed, and uninstall them if necessary.

You can **stop installation** of the current update and restart later if required.

You can turn off automatic updates and **check for updates** when convenient.

If you skipped an update, click **Restore** to receive it.

Windows Update downloads all kinds of critical updates to Vista, including tools to remove **malware** from your PC.

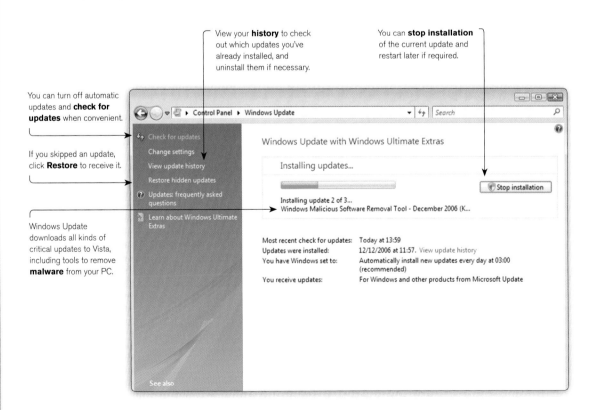

ESET

NOD32. Swift. Nimble. Relentless.

Can you describe your antivirus software
with the same certainty?

NOD32
antivirus system

Just set it and forget it. That's the beauty and the power of NOD32's
ThreatSense® technology. NOD32 proactively protects against viruses,
spyware, rootkits and other malware. And, its high-performance
engine won't slow your system down.

Take a free NOD32 30-day test drive.
Call 0845 838 0832 or download at ESET.co.uk.

WINDOWS XP HAD VIRTUALLY NO BUILT-IN PROTECTION, BUT VISTA COMES WITH
A FULLY FLEDGED SPYWARE SCANNER: DEFENDER. HERE'S HOW TO USE IT.

Introducing Windows Defender

Perhaps oddly, Microsoft decided not to include anti-virus as standard in Vista, but does provide its own anti-spyware program, Windows Defender. Although spyware and viruses have plenty in common – they both attempt to inveigle unauthorised code onto your PC – spyware is explicitly there to steal your personal information.

Defender protects your PC in a number of ways: by scanning it for spyware files, by detecting spyware as it attempts to install itself, and by warning you when something tries to change important Windows settings.

DETECTING SPYWARE When Windows Defender detects a suspicious file, it gives you four options. If you're completely sure the program attempting to run is legitimate, you should choose the 'Always allow' option. If you're fairly sure it's OK, you can choose Ignore. The program will be allowed to install but, should it attempt to mess with important Windows settings, you'll get a second warning. You'll also be warned if the same software is still running when you next boot up Windows.

If you suspect the file is spyware, you can prevent it from running and store it in the Quarantine area, where it will be unable to cause any harm. While it's in this virtual jail, you can choose to restore or delete it. If you're *certain* that a program is spyware, don't bother with Quarantine

– choose the Remove option to delete it permanently. If a program you've allowed to run attempts to change a Windows setting, you get two basic options: Permit or Deny. If you find yourself constantly clicking Permit, consider adding the program to the 'Allowed items' list.

REAL-TIME PROTECTION Defender constantly monitors your system for spyware. It uses 'agents' to check that the Internet Explorer web browser hasn't been tampered with, as well as keeping an eye on Windows add-ons, services, software drivers and applications that behave suspiciously. Internet Explorer is a favourite target of spyware writers. Defender will stop malicious software from changing its settings, such as the homepage, proxy settings and toolbars.

Like most anti-virus programs, Defender can scan your whole system for threats, as well as looking in individual folders. You can choose to exclude certain folders from the scans (removing large folders you know to be clean will save time) by adding their locations to the list in Defender's Settings window – scroll down to the bottom.

By default, Defender is available to every user on your PC. You can disable this by unticking the option labelled 'Allow everyone to use Windows Defender'. You'd only disable it for your own account if you've installed a third-party anti-spyware program instead.

TIP

It can be hard to know if a program is spyware or not. If in doubt, check the website you downloaded it from. Is it the official website for the program you want? Most anti-virus programs scan for spyware too, so if Defender flags up a suspicious file, seek a second opinion by running your anti-virus scanner on the same file. If both programs claim it's spyware, it probably is. Delete it immediately, even if it claims to offer free access to exciting content or pictures of naked celebrities.

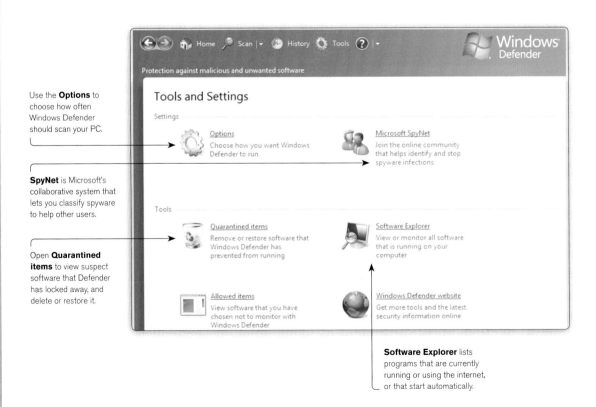

Use the **Options** to choose how often Windows Defender should scan your PC.

SpyNet is Microsoft's collaborative system that lets you classify spyware to help other users.

Open **Quarantined items** to view suspect software that Defender has locked away, and delete or restore it.

Software Explorer lists programs that are currently running or using the internet, or that start automatically.

HOW TO...
DETECT SPYWARE WITH DEFENDER

Scanning and removing spyware is essential if you want to keep your personal files private. Spyware can be irritating at best and criminal at worst. Load up Windows Defender and we'll show you how to check for spyware files and get rid of them.

1 **UPDATE WINDOWS DEFENDER** Before using it to scan your system, ensure Defender is up to date – it will then stand a greater chance of finding the latest spyware. If you have Windows Update set to download and install updates automatically (see p112), you may find it's already updated Defender and you can proceed with scanning straight away. Alternatively, to update from within Defender, click the triangle next to the Help icon on the toolbar and choose 'Check for updates' from the menu that appears.

2 **SCAN** To run a quick scan of your computer, click the Scan icon on the toolbar. This checks the places on your system where spyware is most likely to hide. If you suspect you know where the spyware is, you can instruct Defender to look in one place, which means it will run faster. To do this, click the triangle next to the Scan icon and choose Custom Scan. For the most thorough search, choose the Full Scan option, which checks every file and program on your PC. It will slow down your other programs, though, so it's best to run full scans when you're not using your system.

3 **DEAL WITH THREATS** If the scan finds anything untoward, it will display how many spyware files it's detected and provide an easy, one-button option to delete the threats. If you don't care what they are and just want rid of them, click the Remove All button at the bottom right of the window. If you want to find out more, click the link to 'Review items detected by scanning'.

Each detected file has a list of actions next to it. Choose from Remove, Quarantine, Ignore and Always allow. In our example, we want to move the suspect files to the Quarantine to give us time to figure out what's wrong with them. If you choose the same course of action, make sure you then click 'Apply actions' and not 'Remove all' at the bottom. Once you've dealt with the spyware, you'll probably be asked to restart the computer.

4 **REVIEW DETECTED FILES** To review the files you've detected so far, open Defender's main window and click the Tools icon in the toolbar at the top. Choose the 'Quarantined items' option and look through the captured files. Click any one of these once and a short description of it will appear below. Tick the box next to any file you want to delete, then click the Remove button at the bottom right to get rid of it for good.

HOW LONG?
Half an hour, but could be longer if you have a lot on your system.

HOW HARD?
It's easy to scan, but decide carefully which files to delete or allow.

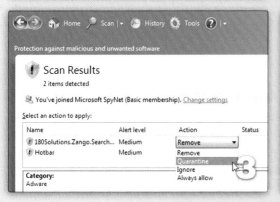

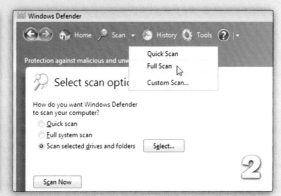

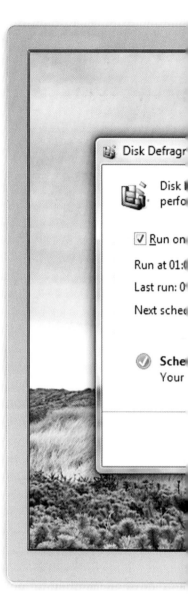

120 Making Vista faster
Learn how to use Vista's monitoring tools to find out what's slowing things down, and make the right tweaks to speed things up.

122 Introducing ReadyBoost
Computer memory is expensive. USB flash memory is cheap. Suddenly someone had an idea!

124 Introducing ReadyDrive
Vista supports the latest hybrid hard disks, another way to put flash memory to good use.

125 How to optimise your hard disk
Our guide to hard disk health, from deleting unnecessary files to defragmenting your drive.

126 Mastering the Control Panel
The old faithful has had a facelift, and gained some new and useful features.

CHAPTER 9

TUNING UP WIND

Vista wants to be the centre of your media and entertainment as well as taking the more traditional PC role of word processor and internet gateway. Accordingly, some of the major under-the-bonnet changes have been about improving its performance and responsiveness. We'll look at some of those features in this chapter, including how to take advantage of a

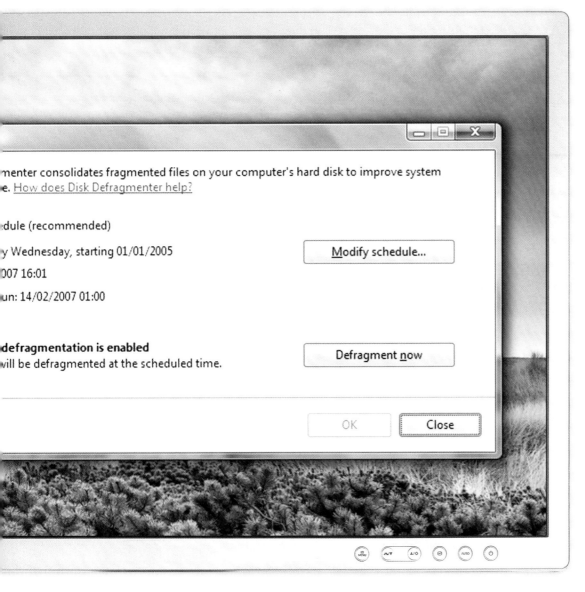

menter consolidates fragmented files on your computer's hard disk to improve system
e. How does Disk Defragmenter help?

dule (recommended)

y Wednesday, starting 01/01/2005

007 16:01

un: 14/02/2007 01:00

Modify schedule...

defragmentation is enabled
will be defragmented at the scheduled time.

Defragment now

OK   Close

OWS VISTA

cheap hardware addition to your computer – a simple
USB flash drive – to instantly boost the performance
of the whole operating system. Once you're familiar
with the basics, you'll also want to dive in and tweak
your system for maximum efficiency. We'll show you
some options in this area too, from mastering Vista's
Control Panel to spring-cleaning your hard disk.

NO MATTER HOW FAST YOUR COMPUTER IS, IT COULD ALWAYS DO WITH BEING JUST A BIT FASTER – AND A COMPUTER RUNNING VISTA IS NO EXCEPTION.

Making Vista faster

HOW LONG?
24/7 – keeping your system up to speed is an ongoing process.

HOW HARD?
You'll need to wield powerful and potentially damaging system tools.

▶ There's a simple rule of thumb for keeping your system running smoothly: don't install software willy-nilly. Think about whether you'll really use it before you clog up your hard disk.

A sure-fire way to make a computer faster is to upgrade it by adding memory, a faster hard disk or faster processor. Vista makes the first of those options very easy with ReadyBoost (see p122 for more on this), but in general hardware upgrades are an inconvenient and expensive first port of call. Especially so when in many instances you can speed up your PC without spending a penny and without taking it to pieces.

What you need to do with Vista, as with almost any other operating system, is tailor the software side of things so that you can apply the maximum resources available to the tasks you want to perform.

COPING WITH LIMITED MEMORY As we've been saying throughout this guide, 1GB of RAM is the minimum we'd recommend for running Vista. A lack of RAM is the single biggest factor that will make your PC seem slow – far more than a slow processor. When Vista runs out of 'real' RAM, it uses the hard disk as a high-capacity but relatively slow dynamic storage area, leading to a dramatic performance decrease.

Using the ReadyBoost feature is one way out of the limited RAM scenario. If you're forced to run with less than 1GB and can't use ReadyBoost, though, you can try to maximise the amount of RAM that's available for

your programs by making sure it isn't tied up doing things you're not bothered about.

Click the Start button, then right-click on Computer in the Start menu and select Properties. The new System Properties window will appear, but we want to delve further than that, so click on 'Advanced system settings' in the left-hand pane. Once you've told User Account Control to allow you to continue, the old-style System Properties window will appear, with an area called Performance. Click on the Settings button and click 'Adjust for best performance', then click OK.

Now be prepared for a shock as Windows Vista appears to turn into a hideous retro monster! The Aero look will disappear, to be replaced by a very old-school angular appearance that predates even Windows XP and looks more like Windows 98. All of Vista's advanced features are still available: they're simply now clad in very drab clothes, which take up fewer system resources. This option may be worth trying if you're very low on memory, and in our tests it saved about 5% of available RAM on a system with 512MB fitted.

You can use the Task Manager to monitor system resource usage (as seen below). Task Manager can be opened by right-clicking on a clear part of the Taskbar and selecting the Task Manager option.

The bar on the left shows the total **CPU load** right now. The graphs show CPU load over time. Since the system here has a dual-core processor, there's one trace for each core.

The more **physical memory** (RAM) you have free, the better. The Physical Memory readout at the bottom of the screen (see below) shows the percentage of RAM that remains free.

Processes shows the number of programs running (and potentially competing for CPU time). Click the Processes tab at the top for details.

Resource Monitor provides a detailed technical breakdown of system usage.

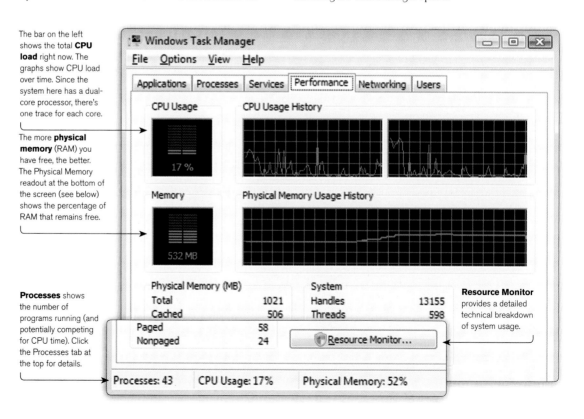

TRICKS OF THE TRADE The second way to speed up a PC is to set it up so it spends less time doing things in the background that you didn't know it was doing anyway and don't care if it doesn't. This can help both with reducing RAM usage and with freeing up the processor (CPU) to give a genuine speed boost.

It may not be immediately obvious, but in a modern and complex operating system – and Vista is the most modern and complex operating system you can install on a PC, by quite some margin – there are always dozens of programs running in the background, even on a brand-new computer with a clean install of Vista that's never been used. If you don't believe us, try this: hit Vista's Start button, and in the Start menu Search box simply type the word 'services', then hit Enter. A UAC box for the Microsoft Management Console will pop up, which you can safely dismiss by clicking Continue. After a short pause, you'll then be presented with a window containing a moderately fearsome-looking list of Windows Vista Services (see right).

A 'service' in this context is a housekeeping task that runs in the background. On a completely clean, virgin installation of Vista Ultimate Edition, there are 116 of these background services, with just under half of them – 52 to be exact – activated and consuming system resources by default.

A note of caution at this point: we're showing you the Services list as an illustration only. Don't attempt to alter or disable services, or your PC may be rendered unbootable. The Services list is genuine under-the-bonnet Windows Vista, and dropping a spanner into an engine is rarely a good way to tune it. Instead, we'll show you a safer route.

DE-FURRING That route is via one of Vista's hidden applications that don't appear in the Start menu. It's called the System Configuration tool, and you can get to it by clicking on the Start button, typing 'msconfig' into the Search box and hitting Enter. Click Continue when the User Account Control dialog box prompts you to confirm your actions, and the tool's unassuming main window will appear. Another word of warning at this point: don't fiddle with this utility indiscriminately, because it can still be dangerous.

What you can fiddle with is the program entries you'll see when you click the Startup tab. On a clean Vista install, there'll only be a few entries in the list, primarily Windows Defender and couple of cryptic ones labelled 'Microsoft Windows Operating System'.

The programs listed here are non-critical background tasks – as opposed to Services, which are often critical – that are set to start up when Windows starts. If you come back to this window after a month or two of using your new Vista PC, you'll find there are many more entries here. This is because a lot of third-party software is written by arrogant people who think their program needs to be running whenever Windows is running. But a lot of the time they're wrong.

To get your system starting up and running faster, uncheck all the program names that you recognise but don't want clogging up your system all the time. Or throw

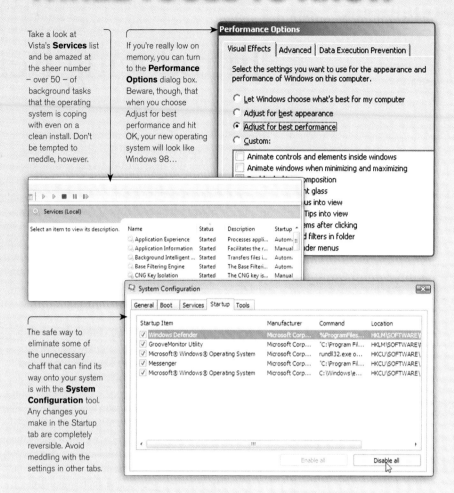

THREE TOOLS TO KNOW

Take a look at Vista's **Services** list and be amazed at the sheer number – over 50 – of background tasks that the operating system is coping with even on a clean install. Don't be tempted to meddle, however.

If you're really low on memory, you can turn to the **Performance Options** dialog box. Beware, though, that when you choose Adjust for best performance and hit OK, your new operating system will look like Windows 98…

The safe way to eliminate some of the unnecessary chaff that can find its way onto your system is with the **System Configuration** tool. Any changes you make in the Startup tab are completely reversible. Avoid meddling with the settings in other tabs.

caution to the wind and hit the Disable All button, then see what happens. You can't mangle your system to the extent that it won't boot by doing this, but of course you should bear in mind that programs like Windows Defender need to be loaded at startup in order to be effective, so by turning them off you're opening up your system to all the internet-borne baddies that Vista's security software was put there to guard against in the first place.

The beauty of the System Configuration tool is that to reinstate a startup program, you just have to recheck the box next to the program's name; or if you want to revert to exactly how things were before you started, just click Enable All and then restart the computer. It's worth noting that you can now perform the same trick using Windows Defender, but the System Configuration tool is a quicker and less fussy method.

Tailoring your background tasks like this frees up the processor and memory subsystems to concentrate on servicing the foreground task – the one you're concentrating on and which is also the one that'll make you angry when you have to sit around twiddling your thumbs waiting for it. The end result is that your system should seem to work faster, even though the hardware is exactly the same as before. Remember to revisit this technique every couple of months to clear up new detritus that's accumulated.

QUICKER WAKE-UP TIMES, LONGER BATTERY LIFE AND GREATER RELIABILITY:
THIS IS THE PROMISE OF READYDRIVE. WE REVEAL HOW IT WORKS.

Introducing ReadyDrive

To describe ReadyDrive purely as a feature of Windows Vista would be to do an injustice to the hard disk manufacturers: they've worked hard on creating a new type of hard disk that will provide numerous benefits. Probably the biggest is that notebook computers will come out of Hibernate mode more quickly.

ReadyDrive takes advantage of the latest hybrid hard disks, which contain flash memory in addition to the traditional magnetic disk. The benefit is that data can be transferred into the PC's main memory much more quickly from flash storage than from the spinning mechanical disk. A hard disk takes several milliseconds just to find the data on the platter (the 'access time'), which may not sound much but can result in the stuttering effect you sometimes get when using a computer.

EVOLUTION, NOT REVOLUTION This isn't a new idea. Hard disks have always had a small amount of solid-state memory – called the buffer or cache – but this is usually only 8MB or 16MB. Hybrid hard disks have a much bigger amount, around 2GB for the first models. Clearly, this allows a far larger amount of data to be stored in the buffer, which means fewer requests for data from the disk itself. The clever thing about Vista's ReadyDrive is that it's designed to take advantage of all this extra buffered data.

We should point out, though, that hard disks are sometimes faster than flash drives. For example, a huge file – perhaps a movie – may transfer very quickly because it's stored in one place on the disk, so after the initial access time there's no waiting. However, mechanical disks are notoriously slow when asked to provide data from random parts of the disk, and this is where the flash memory comes in, delivering the information anything up to 100 times faster. Traditional hard disks, with their small allocation of flash memory, couldn't store enough data in their buffers to make a really noticeable boost in performance, but hybrid disks can.

SIDE BENEFITS If more data can be stored in flash memory, the hard disk can spin down, using less power and prolonging battery life. Also, because the flash memory on a hybrid disk is non-volatile – that is, it continues to store the information even when the power is switched off – Vista can store data on it when going into Hibernate mode, and resume faster when the user awakens the system by reading the data back from flash memory instead of the mechanical disk. Finally, since the disk is used less, it should last longer and be more reliable, and since the disks are stopped more often, there's less chance of data loss if you drop your notebook.

FAQ

Q Will ReadyDrive be available to desktop PC users too?

A In time, yes. Hard disk manufacturers have been developing hybrid hard disks for notebooks first because the benefits are greater. Longer battery life is the biggest advantage; power savings on desktop PCs won't tempt users to spend the extra money on a hybrid hard disk, while notebook users would gladly pay a small premium to work longer between recharges and have extra protection for their data.

A large portion of **flash memory** is the key to the performance, battery life and reliability benefits of hybrid disks.

Mechanical disks are still miles cheaper than flash memory per gigabyte, which is the main reason why there still aren't many 100% flash memory 'hard disks'.

HOW TO...
OPTIMISE YOUR HARD DISK

Over time, your hard disk will get full of applications, documents, temporary files and other data. Unless you keep it optimised, your PC could become sluggish, or at worst grind to a halt. Regular maintenance is the answer; here's how to do it.

1 **CHECK SPACE** Although Vista will warn you when your hard disk is nearly full, you can check how much space has been used at any time. In Computer, right-click on the hard disk icon and choose Properties. If there are several hard disk icons, you should check each one and run the same maintenance tasks as described here on each one. In the Properties window, a pie chart shows the used space in blue and the free space in pink. You can see the exact amounts above the chart.

2 **RUN DISK CLEANUP** Vista needs free space on the hard disk to store temporary files while it's running, so you can't use up every last megabyte for storing data and applications. It's sensible to keep at least 10GB free at all times. If you need to free up some space, try the Disk Cleanup tool – the button to the right of the pie chart. This will search the hard disk to find unnecessary files and, eventually, another window will appear with a list of categories including temporary internet files, Recycle Bin files and offline web pages.

You can quickly see where the most space can be freed up by looking at the figure to the right of each category. But before checking every box, read the description to see if it's wise to remove those files. It wouldn't be a good idea to remove the hibernation file if you actually use the Hibernate mode, for example, since doing so would disable the feature. You can also click the View Files button (where shown) to see the actual files the tool will delete.

3 **EXTRA CLEANUP** At the top of the Disk Cleanup window are two tabs. Click the More Options tab for extra ways to free up disk space. One is to use the Add/Remove Programs tool to uninstall applications you no longer use. The second is to remove all but the most recent System Restore files, but only delete these if absolutely necessary.

4 **DEFRAGMENT** While viewing the Properties window as in step 1, select the Tools tab and click Defragment Now to bring up the Disk Defragmenter options. Over time, any disk will become fragmented: files will be split between different places on the disk. For the best performance, files should be stored in single blocks, and defragmenting does this for you. By default, Vista automatically defragments the disk on a weekly basis, but you can change the schedule or force the tool to defragment the disk there and then.

HOW LONG?
Up to two hours, depending on the size and state of your disk.

HOW HARD?
Doing the wrong thing can harm your system; proceed with caution.

TIP

If your hard disk is still too slow after running Disk Cleanup and Defragmenter, you could add a second hard disk to your PC and get Vista to use them simultaneously to boost performance. Bear in mind, though, your PC will need to have the necessary hardware (a RAID controller), and you may need to buy an identical hard disk to the one you already have.

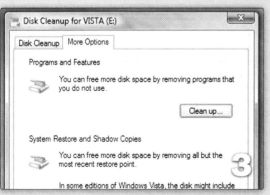

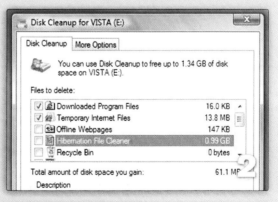

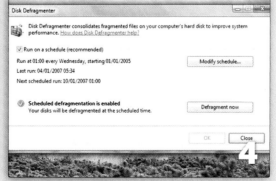

IT'S HARD TO GET COMFORTABLE WITH THE CONTROL PANEL; IN EACH UPGRADE TO WINDOWS, MICROSOFT MUCKS AROUND WITH IT. VISTA IS NO EXCEPTION.

Mastering the Control Panel

Since almost the first days of Windows, stretching way back to version 3.1 in the mid-1990s, the Control Panel has been the centre of Windows' user customisations. With the advent of Vista, there are even more settings and ways of tailoring the operating system to your liking, and fortunately you'll find that the Control Panel's standard view is much better. It all conforms to the standard Vista navigation methods that you'll soon learn to know and love.

A good number of the new entries in Vista's Control Panel are entry points into Vista headline features we delve into elsewhere: for instance, Parental Controls (p110), Windows Sideshow (p142), the Sync Center (p144) and Windows Sidebar (p50). But here we'll drill into a few of the other new categories you should know about.

Although the new default hierarchical view of Control Panel is easy to navigate (see p60), for now we'll assume you've switched to the Classic view by clicking the link at the top left, after you've initially fired up the Control Panel via the Start menu.

DIVING IN Once you've switched to Classic view, you'll see a raft of stylish new icons – some 50 in total. Many will look familiar, such as the trusty Fonts entry that's been there since Windows 95 and rarely, if ever, gets used.

But there are some new and interesting ones that are worth investigating too, some of which could have a real impact on the way you use your computer.

WINDOWS CARDSPACE Windows CardSpace is an intriguing new idea from Microsoft that can only really take off once Vista has reached a certain critical mass, with millions of users worldwide. CardSpace is a way of dealing with your digital identity, and in particular your online identity. That doesn't sound terribly interesting in itself, but it could put an end to the tedious rounds of entering your details for the thousandth time to register on yet another website. Instead, you create a CardSpace identity, which is a secure virtual calling card containing only information you want it to contain.

When a website requests that you register to get access, you simply select your CardSpace card instead (see far right). The interesting part is that you can create and send a number of different cards with varying degrees of information about yourself. So to access a news site that needs basic registration, you'd just send your basic card with your name and email address. But for a shopping site, when you want to make a purchase, you'd select a fuller card containing your street address and credit card details.

TIP

If you want to uninstall an application and you're hunting for the old Add/Remove Programs entry in the Control Panel, you won't find it. It's still there, but somewhat ridiculously it's been renamed Programs and Features, just to confuse you.

Searches that you type here are context-sensitive and will only give matches relating to Control Panel.

There are still plenty of **icons** you'll recognise from Windows XP (and earlier), but Vista also has some intriguing new entries that are well worth investigating.

The old-style **Classic View** is still available, as seen here. (You can admire the new-look Control Panel on p60.)

AUTOPLAY Another entry that could come in very handy indeed is the new centralised AutoPlay tool. This controls the default behaviour when, for example, you put a DVD-Video into your DVD drive or insert a USB flash drive. This default behaviour has always been adjustable by digging around in the right-click Properties menu for an individual device, but bringing it all together makes it easy to get everything set up the way you want it. Double-click the AutoPlay icon and you'll get a clear list of all the categories of media Vista knows about, including DVD movies, games and any drives containing pictures or video, each with a drop-down list so that you can choose what happens when you insert that type of media or device.

OFFLINE FILES The new Offline Files feature allows you to make any files on the network available all the time, even when the network is disconnected. This is done by transferring a copy of the file to your computer. While the network is unavailable, you can continue to view and work on the file, making whatever changes you like. The clever part is that Vista handles all this in the background so that the process should be transparent to the user.

In practice, it's not quite transparent, and you need to make sure your offline file locations are properly synchronised. The Offline Files Control Panel entry is where you should do this. It gives you two main options: to view your offline files and to open Sync Center, where you can set up a schedule for synchronising to the network. The schedule is important, since one of the limitations of Offline Files is that they're not permanently 'streamed', they're synchronised at distinct intervals, which you need to be aware of so you're not caught unexpectedly 'out of sync'.

PROBLEMS AND SOLUTIONS Windows XP introduced the notion of sending error reports automatically when a program failed, and giving you an update if the error was a known one. Vista takes the idea one step further with the Control Panel's Report Problems and Solutions area. This keeps track of any of the program failures that you've sent a report to Microsoft about (by clicking the Send button when a program or driver caused an error or system crash). As well as that, Vista keeps a record of application errors even if you don't choose to send a report at the time; you can use this area to review these errors and check for solutions at your leisure. Note that, by default, Vista automatically sends information about program errors to Microsoft without asking you first. You can use this area of Control Panel to change that by clicking the Change Settings link and choosing the option for Vista to request your permission first.

DATE AND TIME It's hardly Earth-shattering, but while you're in the Control Panel, double-click on the Date and Time icon and click on the Additional Clocks tab. You'll find a neat new entry that lets you add two 'extra' clocks, which you can set to different time zones and name individually. They don't show up on the Desktop, but you can see them by hovering over or clicking on the System Tray's clock readout – ideal if you're travelling with your laptop and need to see what time it is back home.

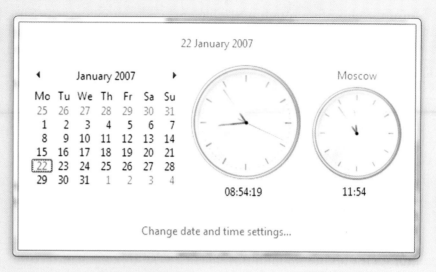

EXTRA CLOCKS One of the many features in Vista that aren't exactly rocket science but which add to the feeling of a well thought-out interface is the extra clock function. You can add up to two and name them individually.

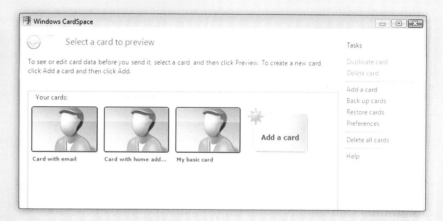

WINDOWS CARDSPACE Windows CardSpace is what Microsoft hopes we'll all start using as a quick and easy way to send only the information we want to websites. You can create as many cards as you like with differing amounts of personal information.

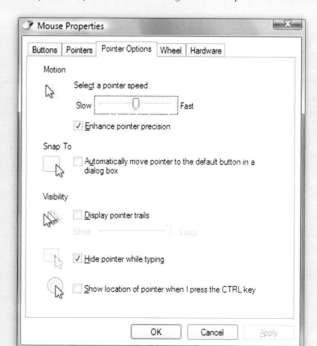

MOUSE SETTINGS
This isn't actually new in Vista, but it's worth pointing out because it's so useful. Double-click on the Mouse icon in Control Panel, click the Pointer Options tab and you'll find some little-known but super-handy mouse pointer options to play with.

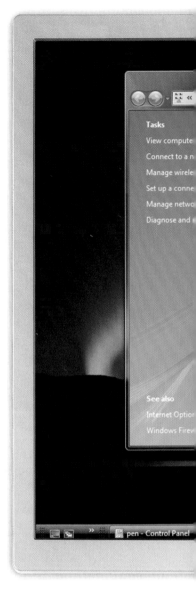

CHAPTER 10

HOME NETWOR

If you have more than one computer, you'll want to share files between them without burning files to CD or filling up flash memory drives. Creating a home network is not only relatively easy, but opens the door to many more benefits than simply moving files from one computer to another. For example, you could store all your photos, music and videos on one

KING

computer, but be able to access them from any other PC on the network. In this chapter, you'll find out how Vista makes networks a doddle. When it comes to more business-like tasks, if you want to share files securely and collaborate on documents with other users, Vista's new Meeting Space also has some clever tricks to make your life easier.

WE'VE YET TO BE CONVINCED THAT PEOPLE WILL ACTUALLY USE IT, BUT MEETING SPACE IS AN INTERESTING ATTEMPT AT A NEW TYPE OF COLLABORATION TOOL.

Introducing Meeting Space

Windows Meeting Space is one of the brand-new applications in Vista. It's also pretty much a brand-new concept, making it difficult to fathom initially and a little tricky to use effectively at first. The idea behind Meeting Space isn't a teleconference or webcam-based virtual meeting, with people in different physical locations. Meeting Space is designed as a way to augment real, physical meetings by allowing the participants to share documents or even applications on their computers and show their Windows Desktop to others. Meeting Space allows other participants to take control of an application on your PC, letting them edit a document or sketch out an idea while everyone else watches on their own screens. A Meeting Space attendee can request control of another attendee's computer or just a single application.

MORE WIRELESS The ideal scenario for Meeting Space is that all participants have a laptop with a wireless adaptor and are all running Vista. That's not a totally unrealistic scenario, since almost all laptops now have a wireless network adaptor built in, but it does certainly limit Meeting Space's usefulness to organisations with the money to equip all their employees with Vista laptops.

One clever feature of Meeting Space is that it doesn't matter if there's no wireless access point in

the vicinity: the Meeting Space clients can negotiate a peer-to-peer, ad-hoc network, meaning there's no extra infrastructure required. This allows you to set up meetings absolutely anywhere, for instance in an airport lounge. Alternatively, you can also use Meeting Space if you're hooked up to a normal LAN (local area network) – there can be a mix of wired and wireless clients in this scenario.

HANDOUTS AND HIERARCHY Meeting Space has some useful ideas. Anyone in a meeting can assign a document on their PC or laptop as a 'handout', and it's then automatically copied to every participant's computer to take away. This avoids everyone requesting emails or paper copies of documents once a meeting's finished. You can also send instant messages to individual participants of a meeting, which will pop up on their screen only.

One of the things that makes using Meeting Space a bit tricky is the very fact that it's based on a peer-to-peer system, with no one person or computer in overall control. Although one person must organise a meeting, they're not really in charge once it's been set up. Handouts can be edited live by one person at a time, but exactly who gets control of the document next can't be decided by a meeting chairperson, so it's a bit of a free-for-all that can quickly become confusing.

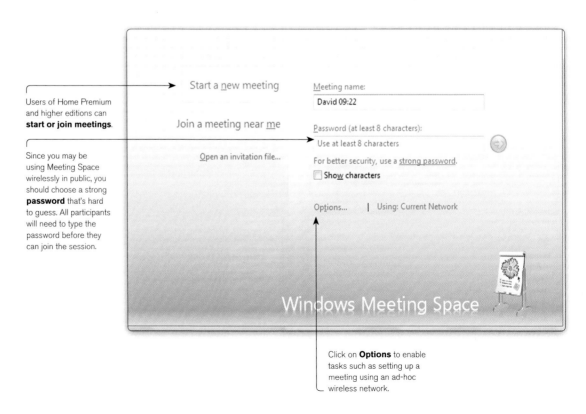

Users of Home Premium and higher editions can **start or join meetings.**

Since you may be using Meeting Space wirelessly in public, you should choose a strong **password** that's hard to guess. All participants will need to type the password before they can join the session.

Start a new meeting

Join a meeting near me

Open an invitation file...

Meeting name:
David 09:22

Password (at least 8 characters):
Use at least 8 characters

For better security, use a strong password.
☐ Show characters

Options... | Using: Current Network

Windows Meeting Space

Click on **Options** to enable tasks such as setting up a meeting using an ad-hoc wireless network.

HOW TO...
SET UP MEETING SPACE

Despite using a wizard, setting up a meeting isn't as simple as it could be. On the plus side, however, the application does at least configure the Windows Firewall for you.

1 **PEOPLE NEAR ME** One of the key aspects of Meeting Space is a supporting service known as People Near Me. For people to invite you to meetings, you need to be signed into this service; it's akin to Instant Messenger, but runs on the local network and doesn't need a server or external account. First of all, you'll need to give Vista permission to sign you in. Since People Near Me can broadcast your presence to everyone in the local area, for security you can restrict its chattiness in the setup box. It's probably a good idea to uncheck the option to sign you in automatically unless you're a habitual user, and you should be particularly careful if you're using your laptop in a public place with your wireless adaptor switched on. As with instant messenger applications, your sign-in name is the name that appears to other people in the area; you can use any name you like.

2 **SHARING FILES** Once your preferences are set and you've signed in, you'll see the main Meeting Space screen (see opposite page). By default, the 'Join a meeting near me' tab is selected; to set up a meeting, all you need to do is click 'Start a new meeting' and enter a password – the meeting name is filled in automatically. The password needs to be at least

eight characters, a reasonably wise precaution given that anyone else in the vicinity with a wireless connection could get access to the session unless your password is suitably hard to guess. Once the meeting has been set up, you can add handouts to the session. A handout can be any file on your computer, which you select using a standard file browser dialog box. As soon as you select a file, it's added to the main Meeting Space view and automatically 'pushed' to all other participants.

3 **SENDING MESSAGES** As with instant messaging, you can send individual notes to meeting participants as the meeting progresses. You can only select one recipient for instant messages at a time, so it's not the ideal tool for briefing your team on-the-hoof in a negotiation meeting.

4 **TIME TO LEAVE** A meeting session doesn't depend on the meeting organiser; once it's been set up, he or she can leave. The meeting will only end when the last participant exits. When you exit a meeting, if you choose to keep handouts they'll remain on your hard disk. Handouts are copied to all computers in the meeting as soon as they're shared, so you won't lose them if their creator leaves the meeting.

HOW LONG?
You can set up a meeting in a minute or two.

HOW HARD?
Microsoft might disagree, but we think it's quite confusing.

TIP

As a meeting organiser, you can make your meeting more difficult to eavesdrop on in public. Before you start a new meeting, click the Options link in the Welcome screen and select 'Do not allow people near me to see this meeting'. Participants will then need to be specifically invited before they can join the meeting.

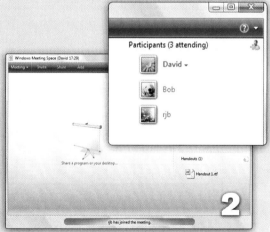

HOW LONG?
You'll need to configure
both PCs, and it can
take a while to sort out.

HOW HARD?
It's sometimes
frustrating – you can
be almost certain
something unexpected
will happen!

HOW TO...
SHARE BETWEEN XP AND VISTA

If you're buying a new computer with Vista installed, you can network it with your existing Windows XP system so you can share files between the two of them. Here's an overview of the process.

Setting up a home network with multiple PCs opens up a host of possibilities for sharing your media and backing up your important files to another computer. If your experience with networking up to now has only been with connecting your PC to the internet, you'll need to configure both your Windows XP system and your Vista system for file sharing. Each folder you want to be able to see across the network will need to be set up as shared.

1 CONNECT VIA ROUTER The first step is to create a network between the two systems. There's no special setup required on the hardware side if you have a broadband router. If both your PCs are already accessing the internet via this router, the network is set up to be able to connect the two computers. For file-sharing purposes, it doesn't make much difference whether the router is wired or wireless.

2 VIEW LOCAL NETWORK On your Vista PC, click the Start button and select the Network menu option. This will open up a view of the computers Vista can see in its local area, which will

initially either be blank or only contain one entry – the Vista PC itself (in our example, it's one called David-PC). We want to configure things so that other computers on the network also appear in this window, meaning we'll then be able to double-click on them and browse files and folders in exactly the same way as browsing around the PC's own hard disk.

3 START FILE SHARING ON XP Moving to the Windows XP PC, right-click on a folder you want to share – we're sharing the My Music folder here – and select Sharing and Security. You'll get a dialog box with two panes catering for local and network sharing respectively. The Network Sharing and Security pane will contain a stern warning about sharing being disabled for security purposes, and you'll see two links. Ignore the one for the Network Setup Wizard, which is a horribly confusing monster of a thing. Instead, click on the one labelled 'If you understand the security risks but want to share files without running the wizard, click here'. If you're worried about that rather long-winded warning, we can assure you there's little need to be, but read our Tip, on the opposite page.

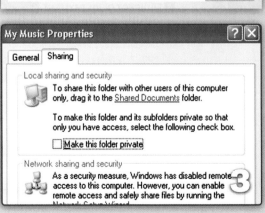

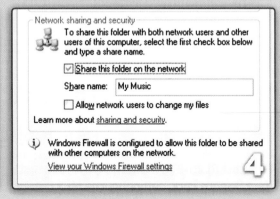

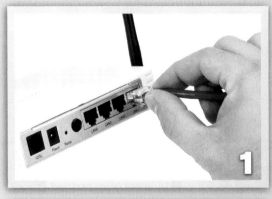

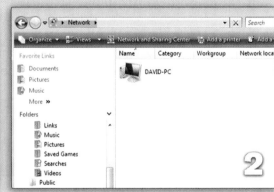

4 CHOOSE A NAME You'll now get yet another warning advising you that you really ought to run the Network Setup Wizard. Ignoring this, click 'Just enable file sharing' and then click OK. The Sharing dialog box will now have changed and contains a checkbox to allow you to share the folder. Click this (contrary to XP's warnings, the sky won't fall in, we promise) and the Share Name text field is enabled, along with a second checkbox. The Share Name is simply the name of the folder as it will appear when you browse it from other computers on the network; you can change it if you like, but there's usually no need, and leaving it the same will avoid any confusion about which folder you're looking at when you access files on this computer from your Vista system.

The second checkbox, 'Allow network users to change my files', is important. Ticking this means you'll give other computers on the network 'write access' to the files in this folder, allowing them to modify or delete the files. Since it's your own private home network, this might not sound a problem. But bear in mind that if you delete files over the network, the operation can't be undone if you change your mind: the deleted files won't appear in the Recycle Bin on either computer. To avoid accidents, it's best to leave this box unchecked unless you really need to be able to alter files remotely.

5 GO TO NETWORK AND SHARING Time to go back to the Vista PC. In the Network window you opened in step 2, you should now click the Network and Sharing Center button in the top menu bar. This is where you can configure Vista to allow it to see the Windows XP machine.

6 ALLOW DISCOVERY Scroll down the Network and Sharing Center window and you'll see the Sharing and Discovery section. To allow your Vista PC to see your Windows XP PC, you'll need to expand the Network Discovery section by clicking the triangle at the right, then click 'Turn on network discovery'. Click Apply, then click Continue when the User Account Control warning appears. Do the same for the File Sharing section and you should be ready to go.

7 REFRESH YOURSELF Going back to the Network window, with any luck you should now be able to see an icon representing your Windows XP PC. If not, hit F5 to refresh the view; it can take a while for the networking system to broadcast the presence of PCs on the network.

8 JUST ONE LAST THING If the Windows XP PC still stubbornly fails to materialise in Vista, try this trick to get connected to it. Click in the Address bar at the top of the Network window (or in fact in any Windows Explorer window in Vista) and type two backslashes followed by the network name of the Windows XP PC – so in our example we'd type \\music – then hit Return. This should kick Vista into looking for the PC and, having found it, Vista should remember it's there in the future.

If you don't know the network name of your Windows XP PC, you can find out easily enough. Go back to the machine and right-click My Computer, selecting Properties and hitting the Computer Name tab. The network name is the same as the 'Full computer name' shown there.

TIP

▶ While you're setting up file sharing, you'll see numerous dialog boxes warning you of the security perils. Remember that sharing folders does mean other people on your private network can see them. It also means a slightly increased risk of a hacker being able to access your PC. The extra risk is small, but make sure you've got encryption enabled if you're using wireless networking (see p70), and of course make sure you have Windows Defender and Firewall running (see p116 and p66).

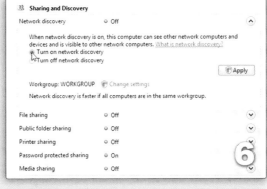

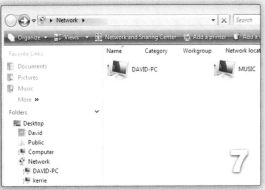

CHAPTER 11

VISTA ON THE M

Vista has been designed with notebook computers very much in mind. In this chapter, we introduce the all-new Mobility Center, which gives instant access to the most commonly used settings for portable computing, such as the brightness of your screen and the amount of power your system consumes. There's also a new and much-improved way to synchronise data with mobile

OVE

devices like PDAs and MP3 players. If you have a Tablet PC, most versions of Vista support it with numerous features, and we'll show you how to fine-tune handwriting recognition. We also introduce SideShow, the new technology behind exciting hardware like the notebook above. And we finish off with a simple guide to using wireless hotspots.

NEW FOR NOTEBOOKS, MOBILITY CENTER BOASTS A NUMBER OF FUNCTIONS.
ADJUSTING POWER OPTIONS TO EXTEND BATTERY LIFE IS JUST THE START.

Introducing Mobility Center

Only available on a notebook or tablet PC, the Windows Mobility Center is a central hub for tweaking the most common mobile settings. It's a small window with a variety of tiled options, most of them familiar. To get advanced options for each tile, you just need to click the icon in the top-left corner and you'll be taken straight to the relevant Control Panel page.

SIMPLE OPTIONS The first and simplest option is to adjust brightness. A notebook battery will run down much faster when the display is at maximum brightness, so try lowering it to halfway and you'll get valuable extra minutes. It's controlled by a basic slider, but changes may not take effect unless you have the latest graphics drivers installed.

Next to this is another slider to adjust the system volume, along with a checkbox to mute the speaker. This is of limited worth, as it's simpler and quicker to click the speaker icon in the system tray. A similar system tray shortcut handles power options, but if you prefer to use the Mobility Center there's a useful quick-select box that allows you to choose Power saver or High performance modes rather than the default Balanced. You can enable or disable your wireless connection from the next tile, and it displays the usual five green bars to let you know the signal strength. Clicking the bars takes you to the

'Connect to a network window, where you can connect to any available networks or open the more comprehensive Network and Sharing Center.

When not on the move, many notebook users prefer to connect to a home or office monitor. With Mobility Center running, plug a display into a vacant video port and click the Connect display button. You may be given the option to extend or clone the Desktop; if not, just click the monitor icon to access the Advanced Display settings. Tablet PC users get an extra option to change the orientation from landscape to portrait.

ADVANCED OPTIONS The final two standard tiles may be less familiar. The first is a link to the Sync Center. Vista Home Basic or Home Premium users can use this to keep files up-to-date between their PC or notebook and other mobile devices; Business and Ultimate editions can also sync PCs, notebooks and devices across a network.

The final tile lets you turn on the extremely handy Presentation mode, changing power settings to disable the screensaver, adjust the system volume and switch the current display background to something more appropriate. The system will always stay awake, and system notifications are turned off. These settings can be further tweaked by clicking the icon.

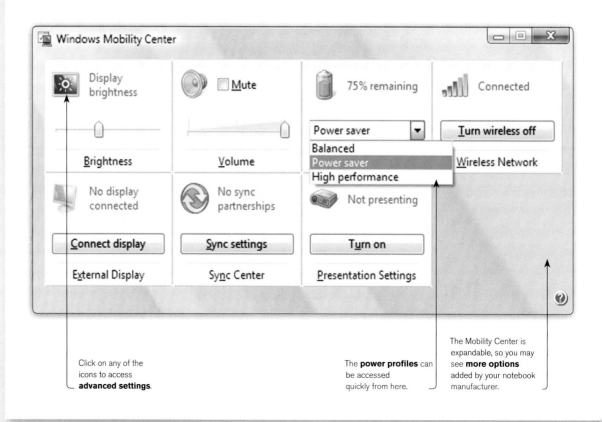

Click on any of the icons to access **advanced settings**.

The **power profiles** can be accessed quickly from here.

The Mobility Center is expandable, so you may see **more options** added by your notebook manufacturer.

HOW TO...
TWEAK POWER SETTINGS

Vista provides an updated, easy-to-find battery meter that tells you at a glance if you have enough battery life left. There's also a comprehensive selection of advanced power options that help you squeeze extra minutes from your battery.

1 CHOOSE A PLAN From the Control Panel, click Power Options (or type 'power options' into the Start Search field). Vista offers three main options: Balanced, Power saver and High performance. Each one simply changes the various power settings accordingly. For maximum energy savings – at the expense of performance – click Power saver. You don't need to apply the setting; Vista registers it immediately.

2 CUSTOMISE Below Power saver, click 'Change plan settings'. Here you can customise the display brightness when on battery power. Since the display consumes a lot of power, choosing the lowest usable brightness will improve battery life, often quite noticeably. You can tweak the amount of time before the display is turned off, and before the computer goes into Sleep mode, down to as little as one minute.

3 ADVANCED POWER You can do more to eke out extra minutes if you comb the Advanced power settings. From this rather uninviting window, you can choose when to spin down the hard disk and the maximum processor state on battery power (reduce this percentage to slow down the maximum allowable CPU speed). You can also force Vista to use every last drop of battery life by lowering the critical battery warning level – set at a rather wasteful 10%, even in Power saver mode – to as little as zero, although you risk losing unsaved work if you have no warning before the battery dies. It's also worth factoring in some spare life to put the notebook into Sleep or Hibernate mode if you want it to wake up quickly next time you open the lid.

4 ADDITIONAL SETTINGS The Advanced settings window also offers many other options. While they won't increase battery life, they can make your life easier. Under the 'Power buttons and lid' section, you can choose the action Vista takes (Do nothing, Sleep, Hibernate or Shut down) when you push the power or Sleep buttons or close the lid. The Hybrid Sleep option lets you decide whether the computer hibernates after a period in Sleep mode. Sleep mode takes around two seconds to wake up, while Hibernate draws less power but takes longer as it must read the data from the hard disk. If you want to disable hibernation, enter 0 then click elsewhere; the 0 will change to Never. Finally, if you use your computer to share media, you can stop it sleeping by selecting the 'Prevent idling to sleep' option in the Multimedia settings entry in the Advanced settings window.

HOW LONG?
Minutes to change your settings, but you may come back to tweak.

HOW HARD?
Easy to pick options, harder to find the most effective ones for you.

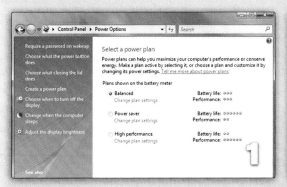

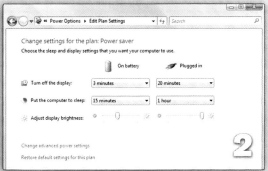

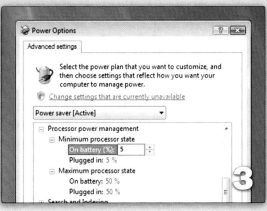

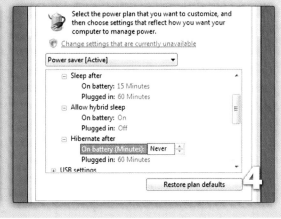

VISTA'S SYNC CENTER GIVES YOU ONE PLACE WHERE YOU CAN SYNCHRONISE DATA BETWEEN COMPUTERS, NETWORK SERVERS AND DEVICES.

Introducing Sync Center

The Sync Center is a new feature in Vista which – like the Network and Sharing Center – provides a one-stop shop for all the controls associated with a particular task. In this case, it's for keeping all your files in sync on all your computers and devices. Windows XP had a basic add-on for this purpose called SyncToy, but the Sync Center in Vista is a much more polished offering.

With the potential for hundreds of gigabytes of data to be scattered everywhere on your network and on mobile phones and PDAs, it isn't possible to keep files in sync manually. Sync Center comes to the rescue, ensuring two or more versions of the same file stored in different locations are matched with each other. If you add, delete or modify a file on one computer or device, Sync Center can mirror this on the same file in the other locations that you choose to sync with, whenever you choose to sync.

HOW IT WORKS When you start a sync, Vista compares the same files in different locations, determines if any have changed (including files that have been added or deleted) and works out which version of each file to keep, then copies that file to the other locations.

By default, Sync Center keeps the most up-to-date version of a file and overwrites the older versions. If the same file has been modified in two different locations,

this becomes a conflict. Sync Center won't try to guess which is the 'right' version, but will ask you which version you want to keep and which version you want to update.

WHAT YOU CAN SYNC You can sync any type of file, including music and photos from an MP3 player, photos from a digital camera, and contact or calendar information if your mobile phone, PDA or other mobile device supports Sync Center. Not all devices do support it, and unfortunately the only way to tell is to plug your device in, install any sync software that came with it, and see if it then appears in the list of new sync partnerships within Sync Center. As with other new features of Vista, support is bound to grow more widespread over time.

One useful way you can use Sync Center is with a NAS drive (see p134). You can update files on your computer and always have the latest versions copied to the NAS drive, where others on the network can view them, or they can be stored simply as a backup. Sync Center can work the other way around too, keeping files up to date on your computer as they're changed on the NAS drive. It shouldn't be thought of as a backup or archive replacement, though: because files are synchronised, you won't always be able to search back and find that older version of a file you now realise you need.

FAQ

Q I'm trying to sync files on different computers but Sync Center won't let me – is there any way round this?

A Unfortunately not, unless you're willing to upgrade the version of Vista that came with your computer. Syncing files with network folders isn't supported by Vista Home Basic or Home Premium; you need Ultimate or Business Edition.

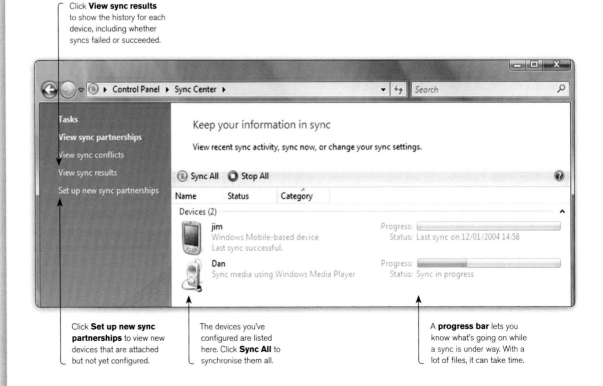

Click **View sync results** to show the history for each device, including whether syncs failed or succeeded.

Click **Set up new sync partnerships** to view new devices that are attached but not yet configured.

The devices you've configured are listed here. Click **Sync All** to synchronise them all.

A **progress bar** lets you know what's going on while a sync is under way. With a lot of files, it can take time.

HOW TO...
SYNC A PDA WITH SYNC CENTER

The Windows Mobile Device Center, part of Sync Center, lets you configure how each of your mobile devices syncs with Vista. For PDAs, you can sync contacts, appointments, email, tasks, notes and more, as well as music and documents.

1 **UPDATE OR INSTALL** To sync a PDA, first make sure that Mobile Device Center is up to date. Either use Windows Update or go to www. microsoft.com/windowsmobile/devicecenter.mspx. If you don't do this, you may still find a Windows Mobile Device Center icon in the Control Panel, but clicking it will only display a dialog asking what interfaces you want to use for syncing (such as USB or Bluetooth). Assuming you now have Mobile Device Center correctly installed, the first time you connect a new mobile device, you'll see two options: 'Set up your device' or 'Connect without setting up your device'. Clicking the latter will take you to an Explorer window where you can view the contents of your device, plus any storage cards.

2 **SET UP YOUR DEVICE** Vista doesn't include Outlook as standard, so you'll need to install a version on your computer if you want to sync email, calendar and contact information. Click 'Set up your device' and you'll see a list of checkboxes where you can decide what to sync. Some – but not all – categories have additional settings, and a link will appear when you tick the box. Click 'Sync Settings' under E-mail, for example, and you can choose whether to download attachments larger than a specified size,

as well as how far back in time to sync emails. Click the Save button once you've made all your settings and you'll be taken back to the Home page of the Mobile Device Center, where a sync will automatically start.

3 **PROGRAMS AND MEDIA** You'll also notice more options have appeared. The Programs and Services tab lets you access your device's Add/Remove Programs Control Panel, and there's also a link to the Windows Mobile website for downloading updates and getting help with problems. The Pictures, Music and Video tab lets you import media from your PDA, and you can choose where to put the files on your computer. You can add media to your PDA from Media Player by using the last option here.

4 **ADVANCED SETTINGS** Roll your mouse over the 'Mobile Device Settings' tab and you'll see 'Change content sync settings' – where you can alter the settings you made in Step 2 – but also a 'Manage a partnership' option. This lets you choose what happens if there's a conflict when syncing: either items are replaced on the device or they're replaced on the host computer. If you make most of your changes on your PC, you'll want to set this to 'Replace items on device'.

HOW LONG?
Apart from downloading the Mobile Device Center, it's pretty quick.

HOW HARD?
Like many tasks in Vista, it's quite easy once you know how.

TIP

▶ To find out if Mobile Device Center is already installed on your system, type its name into the Search bar. If nothing comes up, you'll need to download the program from the web address given in step 1.

HOW TO...
USE WIRELESS HOTSPOTS

The internet is no longer limited to the home or office, thanks to the rapid growth of Wi-Fi hotspots. Be it a café, pub, gym or public payphone, there are thousands of locations that require nothing more than a credit card to get you online.

1 **PRE-PAY** If you know where you're going to be when you go online, you can prepare for it by doing a bit of research. Go to a listings site such as www.totalhotspots.com and enter a postcode to find nearby locations and the providers available at each. You can then go to your chosen service provider's website and either create a pre-pay account or buy a set length of access time before you leave home. Once you arrive at your hotspot, it's a simple case of following step 2, then entering your username and password.

2 **PAY-AS-YOU-GO** If you prefer a little more freedom to roam, you can simply find yourself a convenient hotspot and pay for your internet access there and then, usually on a per-minute or hourly basis. Click on the wireless icon in the system tray, and a small box should pop up to inform you there are available networks within range. Click on that notification and you'll see a list of networks, one of which will almost certainly have the same name as the provider you want to use. In the unlikely event that none appear, you may need to go to Start, 'Connect to' and click 'Set up a connection or network'. Choose to manually enter wireless settings and enter the provider's SSID, selecting 'No authentication' from the drop-down security box.

3 **CONNECT** Click on the service provider's network and you may be presented with a warning screen saying the network is unsecured. This is to be expected, so go ahead and click Connect Anyway, and your system will attempt to connect. Once this is complete, you'll be given the option to save the network, which is only really recommended if you plan to use the same hotspot on a regular basis. If an internet browser window doesn't automatically open, click the Internet Explorer quick-launch (or open your browser of choice) and you should be taken directly to the login page of the hotspot host, ready to enter your payment details and get started. The instructions will vary depending on the service provider, but you'll be offered a choice of payment plans and methods, and the whole process will be self-explanatory.

4 **START BROWSING** Once you've successfully paid for your browsing, a small status window will very likely open, containing the details of your elapsed time, rate per minute or hour and possibly other details such as your username. This will remain open until you finish your session, at which point you may need to remember to click a Log Out button to stop the clock on your payments.

HOW LONG?
A minute or two, but longer if you need to enter credit card details.

HOW HARD?
It's easy, and there are step-by-step instructions online.

TIP

Browsing online at a hotspot can be an expensive business, but there are some free hotspots, and some phone operators (such as T-Mobile) are now bundling free wireless minutes with their packages. Many ISPs offer bundled wireless minutes with a broadband package. Buying credit with The Cloud (www.thecloud.net) allows you to use other companies' hotspots, including BT Openzone, as well as its own.

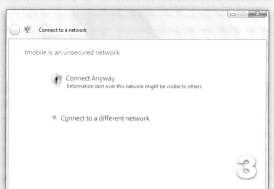

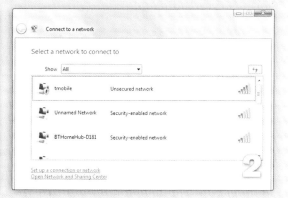

THE ULTIMATE GUIDE TO **WINDOWS VISTA** 147

TABLET PC TECHNOLOGY IS NOW BUILT INTO ALL VERSIONS OF VISTA EXCEPT HOME BASIC. HERE'S HOW YOU CAN TAKE ADVANTAGE OF THE ADVANCED FEATURES.

Introducing Tablet PC in Vista

TIP

► If you'll excuse the pun, this is a TIP tip. On the TIP (Tablet Input Panel), go to Tools, Options to tweak the handwriting interface. You can choose where the panel docks when not in use, to ensure it doesn't block any icons or programs you may be running, select the thickness of ink used in the TIP and the length of pause before entering characters. Plus, you can change the strikethrough gesture type from the basic scratch-out to the old-style Z-gesture, or even disable scratch-outs completely. It's easy to set up Tablet PC exactly how you want it.

A Tablet PC is a notebook computer that you can often operate with a stylus on its touchscreen, without a keyboard. The Tablet PC section of Vista has been redesigned to be even easier to use than the dedicated Windows XP Tablet edition. It all revolves around the Tablet Input Panel (TIP), which looks a bit like an elongated sticky note and is used for all your stylus interaction. When you've finished scribbling, it doesn't close completely, preferring to dock at the edge of the screen ready to be flipped open instantly whenever it's needed again.

The most obvious use for your stylus is for entering text, and the TIP can be used to train Vista to better recognise your handwriting (see right). The more time you spend training it, the more accurate it will become, so it's a good idea to set it up properly before use. But the stylus can also be used for other, more basic interactions.

When you use the stylus like a mouse, tapping on icons and menus to open them, you'll see a big improvement over Windows XP on the visual side. Vista now provides feedback for your stylus, making it easier to see what you're doing. Hover the stylus over the Desktop and a dot appears to show exactly where you are; tap an item and a small ripple appears; right-clicking produces a stronger circle. And these visual enhancements are built

into the basic Tablet PC function, so you won't even need the Aero interface to appreciate them.

FLICKS AND GESTURES The stylus can also be used to carry out other everyday interactions quickly and simply thanks to the inclusion of gestures. There are gestures for Tab, Backspace, Space and many other commands, but they can be changed if necessary. Go to the Control Panel and open Pen and Input Devices for more details.

Another type of gesture, known as a 'flick', is used to navigate intuitively using the pen in a similar way to keyboard shortcuts. A quick flick can scroll a window, navigate a web browser and even perform editing tasks like copying and pasting. Again, go to Control Panel, Pen and Input Devices to customise your own flick for each of the eight main directions, as well as adjusting the sensitivity of the motion. You may need to play around with this until you find a suitable level; click on 'Practise using flicks' to get yourself some extra training in their effective use.

KEEP TAKING THE TABLETS There are two other Tablet PC utilities: Sticky Notes for creating a stack of notes on the Desktop, and Windows Journal for longer notes. The latter can be converted to text or kept as handwriting, and all notes are searchable.

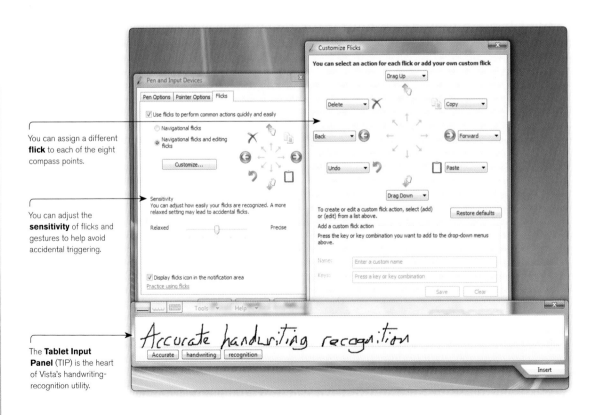

You can assign a different **flick** to each of the eight compass points.

You can adjust the **sensitivity** of flicks and gestures to help avoid accidental triggering.

The **Tablet Input Panel** (TIP) is the heart of Vista's handwriting-recognition utility.

HOW TO...
USE HANDWRITING RECOGNITION

When you first use the Tablet Input Panel, you may be disappointed at its inaccuracy, but you can train it very quickly to your style of handwriting. Like at school, it's simply a case of copying the words and letters with your pen.

1 **START TRAINING** Go to Start, All Programs, Accessories, Tablet PC and click Tablet PC Input Panel. Rather than using the basic input panel, go to the Tools menu and choose 'Personalize handwriting recognition' to begin. While later you might train it on specific common errors, or switch on automatic learning to have it analyse your handwriting automatically, for now choose the option to 'Teach the recogniser your handwriting style'. You'll then be asked whether you'd like to enter full sentences or individual letters and numbers. Choose the letters and numbers option to begin training your system.

2 **EASY AS A, B, C** The wizard will then take you through eight screens to cover all commonly used input characters. The first screen shows you the digits from zero to nine, above a yellow input box just like the one you've seen in the Tablet Input Panel (see opposite page). Just work your way through them, writing the given character in the box in exactly the way you'd normally write it. So if you usually write a small 'a' in a different style to what's shown, do so here to let the system know what it should be looking for. Once you've run through numbers, letters and other characters, you'll be returned to the main menu.

3 **JOINED-UP THINKING** Now that you've told the system how you write individual characters, you should train it to recognise full sentences. Choose that option and you'll be presented with a similar input box, but this time with randomly selected sentences to copy out. Again, you should write the words exactly as you normally would: if you usually join up your writing, or if you write any of the individual characters in a unique way, you should do so here. There are 50 sentences to write, but you can exit at any point and the wizard will add the entered sentences to its training database.

4 **TROUBLESHOOTING** The final option is to target specific problems, such as words or letters that Vista commonly misreads when you write them. If you know which word or character is a problem, you can type it in and write it four times in the boxes to drum the correct style into the recognition system. Alternatively, some written shapes may be interpreted as several different but similar characters, so the wizard provides you with common errors for further training – '0', 'o', 'O' and 'D', for example. Once complete, you should notice an improvement in the accuracy of your handwriting recognition, but ensure automatic learning is turned on to help refine it further as you work.

HOW LONG?
Five minutes for basic training, up to an hour to complete.

HOW HARD?
Very easy – you just have to copy text from the screen.

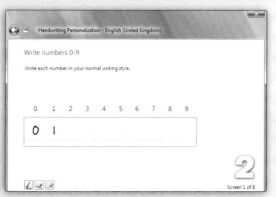

IF YOU'VE GOT A PROBLEM WITH VISTA, THE ANSWER MAY BE RIGHT IN FRONT OF YOU – IN VISTA'S OWN EXCELLENT ONSCREEN HELP AND SUPPORT.

Introducing Windows Help

We've been pleasantly surprised by the quality of the help built into Windows Vista. Most common queries will be answered here, and thanks to its integration with Microsoft's online help – and its support communities – you should also be able to solve more complex problems just by following the links.

The quickest way to activate Help in Windows Vista is simply to press F1. A friendly window will pop up that offers assistance in a number of ways, but you're most likely to choose the very first option, and if you've been paying attention to what we've said about certain themes running through Vista, you won't be surprised to learn that this is Search. This works in the normal way: type in your keywords (for example, if you'd like to change the program that launches a filetype, type in 'change file', without the quote marks) and then press Enter. The 30 most relevant help articles will appear, and you just click on the one that looks most likely.

You'll also appreciate the new guided tours. Entering our example of 'change file' brings up 'Change the program that opens a file' as its third option; click that, and you'll be offered the choice of seeing the whole process take place automatically before your eyes, or you can perform each step yourself, with the relevant part of each screen or menu highlighted as you go.

FIND AN ANSWER Split into six categories, Find an answer is a surprisingly useful way to start learning about Windows – and indeed personal computing as a whole. Click on Windows Basics and you'll find definitions of all the terms common to Windows, and those that are new to Vista. Each article starts off with a basic overview (which may be all you need) and then delves down into the detail.

Security and Maintenance is effectively a checklist of the new security features built into Vista, complete with basic guides on how to use them. Windows Online Help takes you straight to the relevant Microsoft website, and Table of Contents provides a potentially useful way to quickly navigate to the topics that interest you – for example, 'Printers and printing' is one of its categories, which then provides quick links to how to add or remove a printer, find and install drivers, plus many more.

Troubleshooting isn't quite the panacea it sounds. It's really just another way to access the Help articles already there, but with a common set of problems brought to the fore. The What's new category is a little more helpful, giving a decent overview of the features you'll find in Vista – and usefully, they're tailored to the version you have, so if

TIP

▶ When choosing keywords for searches in Help, try to think laterally. What words would you use if you were describing the problem to a friend? Remove common words like 'and' and 'like', then type in what's left. Chances are, something relevant will appear – Vista's Help is surprisingly good at guessing your hidden meaning.

The friendly Help homepage is extremely easy to use, whether you choose to enter keywords into the **Search box** or click on one of the pre-assembled tools – for example, **Security and maintenance** provides a handy summary of all Vista's security options.

you're running a Vista Home Basic PC you won't be deluged with information about the Windows Aero experience, for example.

PHONE A FRIEND Windows XP included a feature called Remote Assistance to allow you to 'phone a friend': if your system was in trouble, an expert could sweep in, take control of your desktop and fix it (for a modest fee, of course). But it was never well promoted. With Vista, Microsoft has brought it to the fore. Within the 'Ask someone' category, the top option is to use Windows Remote Assistance to get help from a friend – or to offer help to someone else. Your friend then gets an email, and when they activate the attached file they'll be automatically linked through to your PC (you have the option to retake control at any time).

Another option is to post a question on the Windows Help community forum. As its name implies, this isn't manned by Microsoft employees, but by Windows users. There are plenty of knowledgeable people out there, and most straightforward queries are answered within an hour or two.

If this still doesn't solve your problem, two Microsoft sites are available. Click Microsoft Customer Support and you'll be taken to the so-called Vista Solution Center. At first this appears to be just a glorified FAQ section, but if you click on Contacts you'll be taken to a page that lists phone numbers to call and allows you to send an email to a dedicated Microsoft support team. There's no charge for the first 90 days after you activate Windows, but a steep £40 (plus VAT) charge per query applies if you go over that period – or if, for some reason, you don't qualify for free support (see FAQ, right).

THE LAST RESORT Microsoft also has an advanced help area called the Knowledge Base. Find it at http://support.microsoft.com/search and you can do a quick search with whatever operating system you're using; enter your terms, press the Search button, and you'll probably be faced with a huge number of matches. The trick is to understand how its keywords work.

For example, if you want to search for a Registry error, you should include 'kbRegistry' in your search text. Other useful keywords are 'kbtshoot', which is in every Troubleshooting article; 'kbhowto', which identifies 'How to' articles; and 'kbinfo', which is in all the articles that just provide general information.

If you still can't find what you want, click on the 'Switch to Advanced Search' link. This opens up a plethora of extra options. If you encounter a specific error message, for example, you can type it word for word, character for character, into the 'For' edit box. Then go to the Using: drop-down field and click on 'The exact phrase entered'.

Deciding what to type in the For box is one of the keys to getting the Knowledge Base to work for you. Unfortunately, there's no easy guide to how to best do it. If you have an error code, type it in, but as the same code can appear in many different items, you'll still need to narrow it down by whatever criteria you can.

IN-DEPTH HELP

USING THE WINDOWS VISTA SOLUTION CENTER You're taken here if you click 'Get your programs to work on this version of Windows'. It sums up common questions, from error messages to getting Media Center Extenders working. It also tackles a number of troubleshooting areas; for example, what to do if you receive a message that your activation period has expired. Click on Contacts to find out how to get support from a real human techie.

USING THE SUPPORT KNOWLEDGE BASE You have to work a little harder to be taken to the Knowledge Base, which is a sensible precaution, as it can be a fearsome place. But it's also very powerful. Click on 'More support options' from the Help homepage, and the Knowledge Base is highlighted halfway down. Click on this link and it will take you straight to the most relevant page, as it's set to only search through Vista-related queries. Then just type in your question, using keywords as normal.

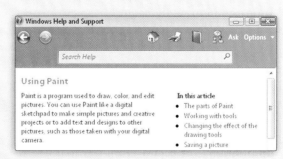

THE 'WHAT'S NEW' GUIDE We like this. There's plenty of practical advice on the bundled apps (good old Paint is seen here). The language is plain but clear, and there are lots of opportunities tig dig deeper if you want to. It's designed for users without a huge amount of Windows knowledge, but even experts may find a hidden gem.

FAQ

Q **I've bought a new computer with Vista pre-installed. Will I get personal technical support from Microsoft?**

A Unfortunately not. You can use the forums, Knowledge Base and Online Help, but you'll have to pay if you want to ask a direct question of a Microsoft techie. This is because Microsoft sells 'OEM' versions of Windows to PC makers at very low cost, with no frills like free support. Your PC's vendor may offer support, though.

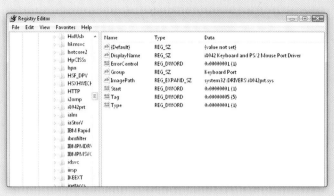

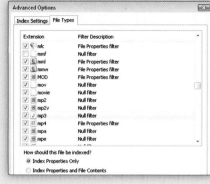

An error in the Registry can cause havoc – so take great care when trying to fix it.

Check your indexing if items aren't found by Search.

HOW TO...
TROUBLESHOOT WINDOWS VISTA

These are some of the problems that have affected Windows Vista during our time using the new operating system. Find your question here and you'll have found the answer – or at least advice on where to turn if more help is required.

Q **I've got a computer that should run Vista's Aero experience, but I don't have any of those swish special effects. What's gone wrong?**

A Sometimes Vista doesn't launch with the 'Aero experience' switched on. However, it could also be that you think your PC supports Aero when it doesn't: it needs at least a 1GHz processor, 1GB of RAM, and a DirectX 9 (or 10) graphics card with 128MB of onboard memory. If you meet all those criteria, first check if your computer's colour is set to 16-bit rather than 32-bit – change this in Display Settings. You also need to change the Desktop scheme to Windows Vista from within Theme Settings. Now open Appearance Settings and make sure Windows Aero is selected in the Color scheme list. Finally, make sure Window frame transparency is switched on: open Personalization, click Window Color and Appearance, and tick the Enable transparency checkbox.

Q **I've upgraded to Vista and now typing is appallingly slow – it takes an age for characters to appear. Sometimes the PC freezes.**

A Nasty. This should only happen with keyboards connecting via PS/2 adapters, or wireless keyboards that use a PS/2 adapter. During the upgrade process a Registry setting was lost, and now you've got to re-install it. Make sure you know what you're doing – changing the wrong Registry setting could severely damage your computer's health. First, open the Registry Editor. Typing 'regedit' in the Start Search box will do this. Click Continue when prompted by the UAC. Now find and click the following Registry subkey: HKEY_LOCAL_MACHINE\SYSTEM\ CurrentControlSet\Services\i8042prt\Parameters.

Double-click PollStatusIterations, then type 1 for the value. Exit the Registry Editor and restart your computer.

Q **Why, when I unplug my USB headphones, does all sound disappear?**

A This affects some USB headphones or microphones, essentially because Vista hasn't detected that you've unplugged them. If it keeps happening, stop and restart the media player whenever you unplug the device.

Q **I'm trying to install Vista, but it's giving me an error message: 'Setup cannot locate a valid hard drive'. I know it's there and working, so why won't the Vista install routine see it?**

A Chances are you're trying to install Windows Vista to a newly formatted partition that doesn't have a drive letter assigned to it. It may also occur if Setup tries to write temporary files to a formatted partition that doesn't have a drive letter assigned to it. You have to make sure that all the hard drives on your computer either have unallocated disk space or contain partitions that have drive letters assigned to them.

Q **I've created a folder in a separate partition for all my MP3 files. I put this folder in the options for Vista's indexing, but it seems the MP3s aren't being indexed. When I put a title of a song in the Start menu's Search bar, it doesn't find the MP3 of the same name. Same with artist names. The same folder also contains a subdirectory with JPEG pictures. They *are* indexed, and can be found with Vista's search. MP3 files in the regular folder (Username/Music) are indexed and can be**

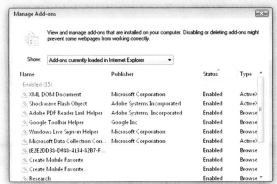
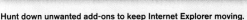

Hunt down unwanted add-ons to keep Internet Explorer moving.

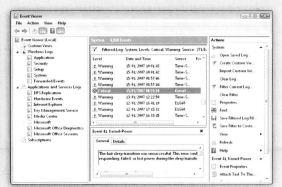

Event Viewer is a professional diagnostic tool that's handy for us too.

TIP

▶ If you install a new device and Vista refuses to start, it could be that you've got a conflict between your new device's driver and another one on your system; it could be a hardware problem, it could be a damaged driver. The quickest possible fix is to remove your new device. But if that doesn't work, head over to the Vista knowledge base (http://support.microsoft.com) and search for article 927525.

found. What do I have to do to get these MP3 files indexed too? The index window in Control Panel says indexing has been completed.

A Check under Advanced options, File Types in Indexing Options and make sure MP3 is checked. Also, there's an option there to Re-Index selected locations, so check this as well. The search facility built into Vista is quite brilliant, but it still benefits from tweaking occasionally within the Advanced Options.

Q My internet browsing has slowed to a crawl. What can I do about it?

A There are any number of reasons why this might happen (physical connection problems, too many people trying to use the same exchange, the website you're trying to connect to might be down), so check the obvious ones first. Try a different website before you do anything else. If you're using wireless, you could have a cordless phone causing interference. You may be sitting in a 'blind spot' for your wireless router, and simply have to move. There may just be some physical obstructions blocking your 'view' – move them, or move your laptop.

Or you may have more serious problems. Viruses and spyware are still common causes of slow internet connections, so do a scan with your anti-virus software and Windows Defender. It's also possible that add-ons to Internet Explorer are causing a problem, so try running it with add-ons disabled to see if that solves it. In Internet Explorer, click Tools, Manage Add-ons. Select Enable or Disable Add-ons, then go through the list. Click on any you fancy removing and select Disable.

Q I bought an OEM version of Windows Media Center that was meant to include a 'free upgrade' to Windows Vista. But I'm being refused. Is there any way around this?

A The OEM (original equipment manufacturer) version of Windows is meant to only be shipped with pre-built PCs from system builders – companies like Dell, Evesham and Mesh. But many OEM copies are sold direct to users by retailers including Amazon (not a well-known PC builder!). They don't come with any support from Microsoft, which is one of the reasons you can buy OEM versions of software for around half the normal price. Unfortunately, Microsoft will only allow its 'free' Express upgrade from PCs that were shipped as an entire system complete with Windows. This may change, though, so check on www.pcpro.co.uk for any updates.

Q I'm plugging in a USB device and it isn't working. What can I do?

A It's not looking good, we're afraid. Windows is set to automatically detect USB devices and install the drivers. It could be you need new drivers and the device manufacturer hasn't yet released Vista-compatible software. It could be there's a problem with the device itself – insert it into another computer to check. It could be that the USB port itself isn't working, so, if you can, use another port, or put a device you know is working into the suspect port. One final possibility is that your device needs power, and the port you're plugging it into can't supply enough. Other ports on your computer may be able to supply more power, or try a powered USB hub.

Q Ever since I upgraded to Vista, my computer has seemed sluggish. What can I do?

A We cover this topic in depth in Chapter 9, starting on p118. You may need to stop some programs automatically starting up at the same time as Windows. You could also change how menus and windows appear, to save processing; again, check Chapter 9 for details. If you're using a laptop, your power options may restrict the processor when on battery power. We explain how to change power settings in Chapter 11. Temporary files can also cause PCs to run sluggishly. Vista has a tool called Disk Cleanup (accessible, as ever, from the Start Search box), which searches for all the files on your disk that are expendable – it can make a surprising difference.

Another more advanced tool is the Event Viewer. It's primarily designed for IT professionals, but logs problems with any Vista system. Click Filter Current Log in the Actions page and you'll see all the Warning logs (and Critical logs, which result in a 'blue screen of death', or Windows shutting down without warning). Any potential problems will become obvious as you browse.

Finally, you may just need to upgrade. Vista loves memory, and you really need at least 1GB.

Glossary

802.11 The name of the official standard that governs aspects of wireless networking and hardware. 802.11b, 802.11g and 802.11n denote the three most common speeds for consumer wireless connections. 802.11b is the oldest and slowest, 802.11g is the most common current standard, and 802.11n is the newest and fastest type, which should become the standard in 2007.

A

AERO Vista's much-vaunted new look, including transparent window frames, live previews of windows and Flip 3D, the updated version of <Alt-Tab> switching between tasks.

ADSL (ASYMMETRIC DIGITAL SUBSCRIBER LINE) The most common form of broadband. It works over existing phone lines once the local exchange is ADSL-enabled.

AGP (ACCELERATED GRAPHICS PORT) An internal slot for graphics cards. Several versions of increasing speed and decreasing voltage were launched. Now superseded by the PCI Express x16 standard, but AGP cards continue to be produced.

B

BIOS The Basic Input/Output System configures your motherboard at startup and boots your PC. It's stored on a flash memory chip on the motherboard itself.

BLU-RAY A form of optical data storage, which (along with its rival, HD DVD), is touted as the successor to DVD. It allows up to 50GB of data to be stored on a single disc – that's nine hours of high-definition video, or up to 23 hours of standard definition.

BREADCRUMB BAR (OR BREADCRUMB TRAIL) Introduced in Vista, this is a new method of showing you which folders you've navigated through in Explorer to reach your present location.

C

CORE/CORE 2 Intel's successors to the Pentium processor, with improved performance and lower power consumption. They both feature dual-core processors (apart from the Core Solo variants), and there are versions for laptops and desktop PCs. Core 2 is the newer, faster version.

CPU (CENTRAL PROCESSING UNIT) Also known simply as a processor, the CPU is the component that interprets and executes computer programs. Common CPUs include Intel's Pentium and Core series and AMD's Athlon and Sempron ranges.

CROSSFIRE Graphics card maker ATi's system for combining the power of two graphics cards in a single PC. See SLI.

D

DDR (DOUBLE DATA RATE) The type of SDRAM memory used in most current PCs, called 'double data rate' because it runs twice as fast as SDRAM of the same clock speed.

DDR2 A faster form of DDR memory, used in PCs made in the last two years.

DESKTOP The primary working area of Windows which, like its real-life counterpart, is the basis for showing your programs and icons.

DHCP (DYNAMIC HOST CONFIGURATION PROTOCOL) Allows PCs on a network to obtain their network configuration

SHORTCUTS
HOW TO USE THIS BOOK

☑ Where you need to **press more than one key** to perform a function, we show this as 'Press <Alt-Tab>'; press the first key, keep it held down, then tap the second key.

☑ When you need to **navigate through a menu**, it's printed in this book as 'File, Save as' or 'Organize, New Folder'. The old XP-style menus are hidden by default in Vista; if you want them back, press the Alt key.

☑ **Internet addresses** are printed like this: www. internetaddress.com. Type them into Internet Explorer's

Address bar exactly as shown. To add a useful site to Internet Explorer's Favorites list, you can press <Ctrl-D>. Clicking Back or Forward buttons is usually straight-forward enough, but lots of Vista's built-in applications use these buttons in an inconsistent way – you'll sometimes find the Back button hidden in the top-left corner, for example.

automatically. On a home network, DHCP is usually handled by your broadband router.

DIMM (DUAL INLINE MEMORY MODULE) The name for the physical package that SDRAM memory comes in (including DDR and DDR2 memory).

DIRECTX A set of Windows extensions from Microsoft to accelerate games and other performance-hungry software by allowing them to use your PC's graphics hardware to the full. DirectX 9 is the current standard for Windows XP; Windows Vista uses both this and the superior new DirectX 10.

DUAL-CHANNEL MEMORY The system used in modern PCs to increase the speed of communication between RAM and the CPU by simultaneously accessing two DIMM modules.

DVB-T (DIGITAL VIDEO BROADCASTING – TERRESTRIAL) A standard used by Freeview digital TV in the UK and supported by digital TV tuner cards and USB sticks for PCs.

F

FAT32 A low-level hard disk format used by older operating systems such as Windows 98 and also devices such as USB flash drives. Vista can also use FAT32, but NTFS is more reliable.

FIREWALL Software or hardware designed to protect networks and PCs from hackers, or from the software they control.

FIREWIRE Also known as IEEE1394, this is a high-speed method of connecting external devices such as camcorders. It's an alternative to USB 2, but more popular on the Apple Macintosh than the PC.

FLASH MEMORY A type of RAM, used in USB memory drives and the memory cards for digital cameras. Flash RAM retains its data even when power is removed.

G

GADGETS Small, usually single-purpose programs that dock to the Windows Sidebar, or can be left free-floating on the Desktop.

GIGABYTE (GB) 1,024 megabytes (MB) when referred to in the context of RAM; 1,000 megabytes in the context of hard disks.

AERO GLASS A feature of the Windows Aero theme, Glass is the effect that makes the borders of windows transparent.

GPU (GRAPHICS PROCESSING UNIT) The chip in your PC, either built into your motherboard or onto a graphics card, that handles 3D games, as well as driving your screen display.

H

HARD DISK A form of reliable, cheap magnetic storage that usually holds all of the data stored permanently within your PC.

HDCP (HIGH DEFINITION CONTENT PROTECTION) A form of DRM (Digital Rights Management) set to be used in the future by high-definition media such as Blu-ray, HD DVD or movie downloads.

HD DVD (HIGH DEFINITION DVD) A next-generation standard for optical discs. It allows up to 15GB to be stored on a single-layer disc

SHORTCUTS
THE MOUSE

☑ When we say **'right-click'** on something, we're talking mouse buttons. Think of the left button as 'select', and the right button as 'options': right-clicking on a file or folder will bring up a menu of your available options.

☑ **'Drag and drop'** is when you use the mouse to move items around the Desktop or between folders or windows. Left-click on the item, hold down the button, and move the mouse to where you want it; to drop it, release the button. If you hold down the Control key (Ctrl on most keyboards) while dragging, you'll create a copy of the item rather than moving it.

☑ In a shift away from the confusing nomenclature of Windows XP, the Start button isn't labelled as such any more. To get to the Start menu, you now need to click on what's officially called the **Vista Orb**, the blue roundel located in the same place.

or up to 30GB on a dual-layer disc – enough for over eight hours of high-definition content. See also Blu-ray.

HDMI (HIGH DEFINITION MULTIMEDIA INTERFACE) A connector designed to carry video and audio signals between high-definition devices.

HDTV 720I, 720P, 1080I, 1080P The high-definition film and television standard, allowing greater resolution and picture detail. The numbers refer to the number of horizontal lines in a picture, and whether those lines are interlaced (i) or progressive (p). Higher numbers are better, and (p) is better than (i).

I

IDE (INTEGRATED DRIVE ELECTRONICS) A hard disk and optical drive interface, largely replaced by SATA, and now common on optical drives only.

ISP (INTERNET SERVICE PROVIDER) A company that provides internet access to customers.

IP ADDRESS A number assigned to a PC on a network to allow it to be identified so that incoming data can find its way to the correct computer.

IPV4 / IPV6 Internet protocols that control the addressing and routing of data packets through a network, such as the internet.

J

JUMPER A small connector that bridges two electrical connections, commonly found on motherboards, hard disks and CD/DVD-ROM drives. Jumpers are used to configure certain hardware settings (see Master, for example).

L

LIVE PREVIEWS An element of Windows Aero, these allow you to see what's happening in a window or application by hovering the mouse pointer over its icon in the Taskbar.

LOCAL FILE/FOLDER A folder or file that's stored locally is on the PC you're using, rather than on a network or another PC.

M

MAC ADDRESS (MEDIA ACCESS CONTROL) A code used to uniquely identify a piece of network hardware. All network devices have a MAC address assigned when they're manufactured. Not related to Apple Mac(intosh). See also IP address.

MASTER A term given to a device on an IDE channel: if there are two devices sharing the same channel, one must be set as the Master and the other as Slave, using jumpers on each device.

N

NTFS (NEW TECHNOLOGY FILE SYSTEM) A hard disk format used in Windows NT, 2000, XP and Vista.

O

OEM (ORIGINAL EQUIPMENT MANUFACTURER) The manufacturer of either an entire PC or an individual component. You can also buy so-called OEM versions of equipment and software, that will come without manuals or technical support.

OPTICAL DRIVE A catch-all term for drives such as CD, DVD, Blu-ray and HD DVD.

P

PATA (PARALLEL ATA) A type of disk drive interface. As distinct from SATA. See also IDE.

PCI (PERIPHERAL COMPONENT INTERCONNECT) A slot used for internal expansion cards, such as TV tuners or sound cards.

PCI EXPRESS A new, high-speed form of PCI, used chiefly by graphics cards.

PPPOA / PPPOE Protocols for connecting an ADSL modem to an internet service provider.

PSU (POWER SUPPLY UNIT) The hardware in your PC that

SHORTCUTS
THE KEYBOARD

☑ Getting to know Vista's keyboard shortcuts will speed up your travels through Windows no end. Pressing <Alt-F4>, for example, will shut down the current window or application, and <Alt-Tab> will flip through all windows you've got open.

☑ You can even use the keyboard to move files around efficiently. Select the files you want – <Ctrl-A> – selects everything in a folder – then use <Ctrl-X> to cut them or <Ctrl-C> to copy them. Navigate to where you want them, then press <Ctrl-V> to paste either the original items (if you cut them) or a copy of them into this folder.

☑ If you've got a scroll wheel on your mouse, hold down the Control key and use the wheel to zoom in and out. It works in most applications, including Internet Explorer and Microsoft Word. It even works on the Desktop or in Explorer windows, where it scales the size of icons.

connects to the mains and supplies power to the PC's motherboard and internal components.

R

RAM (RANDOM ACCESS MEMORY) A high-speed form of memory, holding the data and documents that you're currently using. The content of RAM is lost when the PC is switched off (except in the case of flash RAM).

READYBOOST A method of using cheap USB flash drives to boost the speed of PCs with less than 1GB of RAM.

RSS (REALLY SIMPLE SYNDICATION) A standard for publishing dynamic information, such as news feeds, which can be read by various applications, including Internet Explorer 7.

S

SATA (SERIAL ADVANCED TECHNOLOGY ATTACHMENT) A form of data connection used by modern hard disks.

SAVED SEARCHES Folders that contain a set of user-defined search results, which update dynamically as files matching the criteria are added.

SDRAM (SYNCHRONOUS DYNAMIC RAM) The memory technology fitted to most PCs for the last five years.

SIDEBAR The area to the left or right of Vista's Desktop that plays host to Gadgets.

SHADER MODEL A graphics technology used to describe and render scenes in games.

SLAVE See Master.

SLI (SCALABLE LINK INTERFACE) Nvidia's method of linking two graphics cards, theoretically capable of producing twice the performance of a single card. See also CrossFire.

SODIMM (SMALL OUTLINE DUAL INLINE MEMORY MODULE) A reduced-size RAM module used in laptops.

SYSTEM TRAY A small area of the Taskbar used to show volume settings, network status, and other applications that are running but don't have a Taskbar button.

T

TASKBAR Arranged by default along the bottom of the screen, the Taskbar is home to the system tray and Start button, as well as the icons of programs that are currently running.

TCP/IP (TRANSMISSION CONTROL PROTOCOL/INTERNET PROTOCOL) A set of protocols used to transmit data over networks; the fundamental protocols at the heart of the internet.

U

USB (UNIVERSAL SERIAL BUS) A 'plug and play' standard for connecting the vast majority of peripherals to a PC.

USB 2 The fastest form of USB currently available, running at speeds of up to 480Mb/sec. Also known as Hi-Speed USB. 'Full-Speed' USB, also known as USB 1.1, runs at a much slower 12Mb/sec.

W

WAN (WIDE AREA NETWORK) A network that extends over a large geographical area, as opposed to a LAN (local area network). A broadband modem's external port is labelled WAN.

WEP (WIRED EQUIVALENT PRIVACY) A common, but flawed, method of encrypting the data sent over a Wi-Fi connection. It gives fair protection but can be broken by a determined eavesdropper.

WI-FI The generic term for wireless 802.11a/b/g/n networks and connections.

WPA (WI-FI PROTECTED ACCESS) A very secure method of encrypting the data transmitted on a wireless network. WPA is more secure than WEP, but some older hardware doesn't support it. The WPA2 standard is even tougher again.

SHORTCUTS
THE WINDOWS KEY

☑ One of the most powerful keys in Vista is the Windows key. It's generally found at the bottom left of most modern keyboards, although it may be elsewhere on laptops.

☑ Pressing the Windows key by itself will take you straight to the Start menu's Search box. Start typing the name of an application (such as 'word') and Vista will narrow down the search results with each letter you type. Once you've got the application you want, hit the Enter key to run it.

☑ Pressing the Windows key with D minimises everything to get you back to the Desktop, <Windows-Space> brings the Sidebar and any open Gadgets to the front, and <Windows-F> brings up an Instant Search window: you can then search your indexed folders without even having to reach for the mouse.

Win a Sony VAIO!

Sony has updated its range of VAIO notebooks to embrace Windows Vista, and the results are impressive. There's the all-new G11, a 1.13kg notebook with a DVD writer and 100GB hard disk. And it lasts for up to nine hours per charge – simply amazing. Or the stunning new C2 series, which ranges in colour from Free Spirit Pink to Rediscovery Blue!

WHAT YOU COULD WIN One very lucky reader will walk away with a VAIO SZ4VWN, exclusive to Sony Style. This includes a 3.5G card, allowing you to send email, update files and keep in touch with colleagues at broadband speeds. You can even try the T-Mobile 'Web 'n' Walk' package for 30 days without charge.

The SZ4 includes a generous 13.3in widescreen and weighs from just 1.69kg, plus it offers up to six hours of battery life per charge. The lightweight carbon-fibre chassis not only saves pounds but also protects the powerful components inside.

The model we're giving away features an Intel Core 2 Duo T7400 processor, 160GB hard disk, 2GB of RAM and Nvidia's GeForce Go 7400 graphics. A thoroughbred business notebook for the complete professional, the SZ4 series includes a fingerprint reader and a Trusted Platform Module for extra security. With Windows Vista Business installed, you also benefit from enhanced backup and networking tools.

VAIOS FOR EVERY NEED For the complete VAIO range, visit www. sonystyle.co.uk or find more details in PC Pro's 20-page ezine (see below right). Highlights include the N29, a great-value business notebook at £769 including VAT, and the TX5, a compact notebook that weighs just 1.25kg and features a widescreen display and DVD writer.

For a truly revolutionary product, take a look at the UX1. This weighs less than half a kilo, yet it's a fully fledged Windows Vista PC. With a 32GB flash disk, it's lighter and more compact than any other Ultra Mobile PC, and integrates a sliding keyboard for easy writing on the move.

DON'T MISS YOUR CHANCE...

To enter, go to www.pcpro.co.uk/links/sonycomp and answer the following questions:

1. The SZ4VWN includes a 3.5G card. But what does the 3.5G card allow you to do?
(a) Browse the internet at dial-up modem speeds   **(b)** Browse the internet at broadband speeds
(c) Encrypt data on hard disks

2. The 3.5G card comes with a certain number of days' free subscription to T-Mobile's 'Web 'n' walk' package, covering all data costs (UK only). But how many days?
(a) 10 days **(b)** 20 days **(c)** 30 days

3. What advantage does Sony Style offer over any other online retailer of Sony products?
(a) Exclusive models and pre-ordering of new ranges
(b) Expert advice from a team that only deals with Sony products
(c) Both of the above

ABOUT SONY STYLE

Browse through the variety of Sony ranges using this dedicated **navigation bar**.

Exclusive offers and promoted items are clearly displayed on the Sony Style home page.

Click here to switch to a dedicated **business site**.

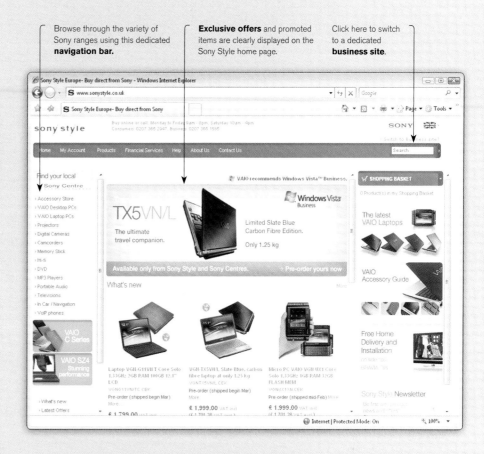

EXPERT Sony Style was set up for one reason: to sell Sony products direct. Because staff only deal with Sony products, they know every detail and can provide truly expert advice. Including which version of Windows Vista, and which VAIO, is right for your needs.

FIRST As soon as the latest Vista-enabled Sony VAIO is released, you can buy it first from Sony Style. What's more, to make absolutely sure you're the first to receive the latest technology, you can pre-order notebooks via the Sony Style website (above) or over the phone.

EXCLUSIVE Thanks to its direct links with Sony, Sony Style can offer its customers a number of exclusives – including the Sony VAIO SZ4VWN we're giving away here. There are also exclusive bundles and many more special edition notebooks.

Visit www.sonystyle.co.uk today, or call for expert advice on 020 7365 2798.

HOW TO...
GET A VISTA EZINE

PC Pro has produced a complimentary 20-page ezine all about Windows Vista and Sony's new range of VAIOs. To see a video of the phenomenal new G11 in action and an exclusive video interview with David Weeks (UK marketing manager for Windows Vista), and for more details of all the latest VAIOs, visit www.pcpro.co.uk/links/sonyezine.

Index

THE ULTIMATE GUIDE TO WINDOWS VISTA

EDITORIAL

Editor
Tim Danton
editor@pcpro.co.uk

Managing Editor
Adam Banks

Contributing Editors
Ross Burridge,
David Fearon

Contributors
David Bayon, Simon
Edwards, Jim Martin,
Dave Stevenson,
Alex Watson

Design and layout
Vast Landscape
info@vastlandscape.com

Production
Dharmesh Mistry, Alex
Milway, Jo Clements

Photography
Danny Bird,
Alessandra Chilá

Cover Illustration
Richard Osley

ADVERTISING

Advertising Manager
Julie Price
020 7907 6660

**Advertising
Production**
Fax 020 7907 6066

Operations Director
Robin Ryan

Marketing Manager
Claire Childs

Competition Manager
Emma Winfield

PRINT

Printed by BGP, Bicester,
Oxfordshire

**INTERNATIONAL
LICENSING**

PC Pro content is
available for licensing
overseas. Contact Richard
Bean, International
Licensing Director
00 44 20 7907 6136
licensedir@dennis.co.uk

MANAGEMENT
020 7907 6000

Publishing Director
Ian Westwood

**Group Advertising
Director**
Julian Lloyd-Evans

Circulation Director
Martin Belson

Finance Director
Brett Reynolds

**Group Finance
Director**
Ian Leggett

Chief Executive
James Tye

Chairman
Felix Dennis

A DENNIS PUBLICATION

Dennis Publishing Ltd,
30 Cleveland Street,
London W1T 4JD.
Company registered in
England. All material ©
Dennis Publishing Limited
licensed by Felden
2007, and may not be
reproduced in whole or
part without the consent
of the publishers. ISBN
0-9548577-6-3

PERMISSIONS

Material may not be
reproduced in any form
without written consent
of the publisher. Please
address such requests
to Ian Westwood, Dennis
Publishing Ltd, as above.

REPRINTS

PC Pro operates an
efficient commercial
reprints service. For
details please call
020 7907 6620

LIABILITY

While every care was
taken during the
preparation of this
bookazine, the
publishers cannot be
held responsible for
the accuracy of the
information or any
consequence arising
from it. All judgements
are based on equipment
available to Dennis
Publishing at the time
of review. 'Value for
money' comments are
based on UK prices at
the time of publication.
Dennis Publishing
takes no responsibility
for the content of
external websites whose
addresses are published.